DEATH AND HAM

LIFE IS A REAL TRIP

My Best,

Bobby Evers

BY
BOBBY EVERS

Death and Ham: Life is a Real Trip
Copyright © 2022 Bobby Evers

Published by Berger Street Press

For more information : www.shoesandcheese.com

All rights reserved. No part of this book may be used or reproduced in any form or by any means, electronic or mechanical or in performance, including photocopying, recording, or any information storage and retrieval system without express written permission from the author.

ISBN 978-1-7374175-3-8

First Edition

10 9 8 7 6 5 4 3 2 1

Editor: Wordsmith Collaborative, Nashville, TN
Cover Graphics: Meltmama Creative Studio
Original Cover Artwork: Bobby Evers . All rights reserved.

To Nell

DEATH AND HAM
LIFE IS A REAL TRIP

Introduction	1
Death and Ham	3
In Training	9
Not the Bird…Again	19
A Cruise? I'll Take Mine Nude	27
Monkey Business	37
Nashville Is It!	45
Coffee Culture	55
Outta Space	63
Table for One	71
At Wit's End	83
Paris at Night	89
Quality Time	97
My Style	117
Trials and Tribulations	127
Ode to Savannah	137
The Flat Tire	149
All in the Big-Headed Family	165
The Grand Scheme of Things	179
Travel Plans	185
I Want to Be a Part of It	195
Suddenly, A Writer	207
Then and Now	213
The End	225

INTRODUCTION

At a certain age, you take off the rose-colored glasses. You see things for what they really are. I think that's why I prefer watching *Dateline* and *Forty-Eight Hours* over *CSI*. I want the real stories, not fictionalized ones.

I also prefer reading biographies over novels. And I always choose live theater rather than seeing a movie or video because it's happening right *there*, in front of you, without edits and camera angles and Photoshop. Theater is not *TikTok*, and that's fine by me.

But most of all, I like people who are the real deal. No fake personas or wishy-washy types for me. I like to know where I stand and who I can trust. I want to know who I can call when I need to hide the body—or when I find one in my air vent.

I like that I've been around long enough to know a few things about myself too. I know that I'm only going to be happy if I'm doing something creative and juggling a few projects. I also know that some people will get my humor while some will glaze-over at hearing one of my stories—and I'm good with that.

My tolerance for nonsense is much lower these days, and I really like that as well. Life is just too short to deal with a bunch of crap. I hate serving on

Introduction

committees and going to meetings too, because they generally involve the aforementioned *bunch of crap*.

For me—at sixty—the ironies really start to add up. As my list of doctor appointments grows longer, my memory only gets shorter. I have more time to go on trips, but less energy to expend on those trips. And there is new technology to help me do just about anything but, sadly, I can't figure out how to use most of it.

And it's also sad that it takes most of our lives for many of us to get comfortable in our own skin. Maybe that's why we sag and wrinkle as we age. All that squirming around inside—trying to figure out exactly who we are—does tend to stretch out the skin a bit and leave some marks.

That's ok, though. I'll take some wrinkles in exchange for all the wisdom gained, and I'll try to smile when I look at my older self in the mirror. Because really the only good way I've found to combat aging—other than death, and that kind of defeats the whole purpose—is to laugh at it. What other choice do we have?

In my stories you'll find some of the people and places that have inspired me and kept me smiling.

I hope they leave you with a smile too.

DEATH AND HAM

Someone died. I can't remember exactly who. So a friend and I decided we should send food.

I am not sure about the rest of the country, but in the South if you die your family gets lots of food. Someone usually brings ham. Pies are big, and Bundt cakes are making a comeback. Really, when you think about it, it just makes sense. After all, a squash casserole is really the only logical replacement for Aunt Gertrude.

So, on this particular occasion, I was in Nashville and planning to drive down for *someone's* funeral. I told my friend I would stop by the designer ham store near my place. I guess I should not share the actual name of the store, so I will just call it Sweet Roasted Hams. I thought I would purchase enough ham for ten or twelve people and drop it off at the home of my grieving friends. I figured twenty-five or thirty dollars would cover it.

Not that I was particularly worried about the cost. Back in Boonetown, you could go by the barbecue place and easily get enough smoked ham to feed twelve people for less than twenty-five bucks. I knew this ham store's would cost more than that, being in Nashville and all. But I didn't think it would cost all that much more.

As soon as I entered, though, I realized I had completely mis-assessed the situation.

I felt like I had entered a jewelry store, not a deli. There was a well-dressed clerk behind the counter who interviewed me prior to my purchase. He wanted to know the purpose of my visit and if I would be acquiring just the ham, or if I would need a complete meal. I told him I was just in the market for some ham—enough to feed ten or twelve folks.

He turned, much like Vanna White, and caressed a case filled with gold-foil-wrapped hams. Scanning the labels, he found one he thought would be appropriate for me and proceeded to gently take it from the case and place it on the counter. Then he carefully removed the gold foil and displayed the ham for me to peruse. Just like at a jewelry store, you cannot remove the merchandise from the case without assistance. A Sweet Roasted Ham must be removed from the cooler by the clerk. You also cannot touch them after he lays them on the counter. He then pointed out the features of the ham: the marbling, the color, the texture—much like a jewelry salesman would point out the cut and clarity of a fine diamond. By this time, I knew I was in the Tiffany & Co. of meat shops, and the prices were comparable.

As any good jewelry salesman would, he began by showing me something larger than I had indicated I wanted. We were well above the hundred-dollar mark for this little beauty. I say little because it seemed quite small for the price. I hated to sound cheap, but I asked if I could see something a little less expensive. He looked a bit disappointed in me. Then he carefully refolded the gold foil and placed it back into the cooler. He removed another ham. I think this one was down around eighty dollars. It looked pitiful, this little mass of ham that cost more than a full catered meal. But I knew I couldn't take any less ham to my friend without looking like a total cheapskate. I was just hoping that my friend had shopped at Sweet Roasted Hams before, so they would know that I had spent a respectable amount of money.

The clerk said I would really need one at least this big to feed a dozen, so I said I would take it.

The care with which he re-wrapped it and placed it in a bag made me feel that I was, indeed, purchasing something like a diamond ring—that I would want to keep for a lifetime. I felt compelled to drive much more carefully on the way home. I was carrying precious cargo, and it needed to be delivered to the mourners unblemished.

Going to funerals is something that I never enjoy— I'm sure no one does. But I can honestly say that I would just as soon go to a funeral as to one of the other great rituals of life: a wedding. I know they are supposed to be joyful occasions, but I just can't seem to find a way to enjoy them. At least at the end of the funeral you know how everything turns out. A marriage takes years to unfold. And, generally, at a funeral, no one tries to force you onto a dance floor.

And didn't weddings used to happen in a church? Every wedding I can remember did. Then, all of a sudden, weddings started having to take place at a "venue." The venue often turns out to be a barn, or a museum, or maybe on a pier over water, or out in a field in front of a pair of old salvaged doors—that last one has really become popular. It seems the odder the venue, the better.

One of my friends booked a large cave for their wedding festivities, which I thought was really cool. But then it flooded and they had to move it. I guess now I'll never know what that might have been like.

Suddenly, even Boonetown has more wedding venues than I can count. It seems a church is now the absolute last place anyone wants to get married.

At least churches and reception halls come with restrooms. When you are stuck out in a field somewhere, who knows where the nearest relief station might be? (As I get older, restroom proximity has become a bigger and bigger consideration when deciding which events I will attend.)

At many of these new venues, parking is usually an issue too.

And another big challenge is figuring out what you should wear. I used to always wear a suit to a wedding. But now I find I am often more dressed-up than the wedding party. So I've even had to rethink that. It's all just a bit too stressful.

Funerals, for the most part, still seem to be holding to their accepted patterns. Funerals are still happening in the traditional locations: funeral homes, churches, and, of course, cemeteries. Black clothing is still good. And, like always, funerals are just one more reminder of the inevitable aging process. As you get older, you go to more and more of them, until the last one you attend—your own.

I've talked to a surprising number of people who seem to be quite concerned about how many people will show up at their own funeral. It's really kind of out of your hands at that point, I think. But still, some people seem to be very concerned. Of course, the younger you are, the more mourners you will likely have, since most of your friends are still alive.

If you have a big family, that will definitely help ensure a crowd—assuming you are on good terms with all of them. But, of course, the day of the week and the proximity of your funeral to a holiday can definitely affect attendance. I guess one should plan *when* to die accordingly.

My oldest nephew told me he is leaving money in his estate to pay a crowd of mourners to gnash their teeth and wail and sob loudly, just in case there isn't sufficient gnashing of teeth and wailing from the real mourners. He said he definitely doesn't want "any of this *celebration-of-life* bullshit." He wants old fashion despair and anguish. So, in his case, keeping mourners on retainer seems like a good plan because, you never know, you might die during spring break and lose a lot of mourners to the beach.

Over the years, I've carried a lot of caskets, and I've lost a lot of important people. No matter the type of funeral, I don't think there is any good way to say that last goodbye. You just sort of have to get through it. One lesson I have learned, though, is that it takes death to appreciate life.

We buried my brother last year. He was way too young. He didn't take care of himself and his diet was terrible, so it wasn't a total surprise. But it's still a shock to lose someone at sixty-three. His funeral was crowded with many family members and friends, all stopping by to extend their sympathy.

Both of his sons spoke, and they shared many funny stories about their dad. Everyone was able to laugh a lot and to grieve as well. It really was a kind of celebration. And it was something I think he would have approved of—and he didn't approve of much when it came to ceremonies and such. He liked to keep things simple, to the point, and with little fanfare.

It did make me think a little about what I might want at my own funeral. Certainly not sobbing and gnashing of teeth. Well, maybe just a little. But what I would really want is lots of family and friends gathered together and laughing a lot.

That's my favorite thing about life: laughing with people I love.

Maybe they will read a story or two of mine as well.

And maybe someone will bring some ham.

I hope they spring for the good stuff.

IN TRAINING

Lately, I have begun to feel a deep resentment for Ricco. It started slowly. And, like a boil, it has been growing and festering under my skin. I'd like to say that this resentment is reasonable, but it isn't.

I pay this person to come into my home. I could just as easily discontinue him, but this is good for my health—I am told—and my doctor thinks it's a very good thing.

It all started off innocently enough. I had been going to the gym for twenty or so years, ever since I began living in Nashville part-time.

Of course, it took me a few years to make the big decision and finally join the YMCA. When I first started even *thinking* about joining a gym, I was really concerned that I would look like a total weakling. So, like the people that clean their house before their maid comes, I bought a Soloflex machine. I worked out at home for a year or so before I made the leap to the actual gym.

I was very dedicated at first, spending a lot of time on the machines and then doing cardio. I could see some improvements in my appearance too, so that made it worth the trouble.

I had been emotionally scarred by my experiences in high school gym class. My less-than-great coordination and lack of interest in sports made me *real* popular with the other boys. They all thought I should at least be good at basketball, since I was very tall.

They were wrong.

I was painfully skinny too, and I hated all the locker room insults and the showers. You name it, anything associated with gym class, I loathed. For me, gym class was one hour of torture to be endured each day and something to be dreaded the other twenty-three.

So it was no surprise that, by the end of freshman year, I swore I would never enter another gym for the rest of my life.

After the passing of a couple of decades, though, here I was, at a gym—actually working out. I certainly didn't *love* it, but I didn't hate it. It was even fun some days. Especially when I got to know a lot of the guys. They were actually nice, not like some of the assholes I went to high school with. So at least I was making some pleasant memories to blur all the bad ones from high school.

As the years progressed, though, I became bored with my workouts. I began to lose interest and motivation. I was finding excuse after excuse not to go to the gym. The parking. The traffic. The busy time. The slow time. Too soon after a meal. Too tired. You name it, I would use it as an excuse.

The people all sort of began to run together too. They were all so predictable that I came up with my own classification system. The *posers*. The *socialites*. The *hardcore lifters*. And of course, the *residents*.

The *residents* were really fascinating to me. I went to the YMCA for close to twenty years and there were a few guys that, I swear, I saw there every time I went. Every single time. Did they have a life outside of the gym? I wondered.

Many of the guys I called the *socialites* liked to stop by the gym after work or at lunch, just to visit and chat with their buddies. I never saw many of them ever get in much of a workout. They were mostly leaning on the machine of someone who was actually working out, talking to them. They did much more talking about their workout than ever actually doing it.

The *hardcore lifters* were all business. They often looked like Sumo wrestlers, and spent all their time in the free weights, grunting and lifting.

The *posers* were by far the most entertaining. It seemed like every set of reps they did was followed by at least five minutes of mirror time—flexing, posing, primping. Fortunately, most gyms are full of mirrors, so they didn't have to go far for one. They loved to look at their muscles, and it's pretty obvious they wanted everyone else to look at them too. They often had trouble keeping any clothes on in the locker room. They loved to strip-down, go weigh on the scale, take another post-workout look in the mirror, maybe take a selfie or two, and get a protein shake— all while wearing just a towel, or less. I supposed their muscles were bulging so much it was difficult to keep a towel wrapped around them. They loved being observed. And if you ever wanted a two-hour presentation on the benefits of weightlifting, just ask one of them about their workout routine.

But I was kind of sick of all the gym-types. I burned

out on the gym.

I worked out at home when I could motivate myself to do so. But that wasn't happening much either. And even when I did, it took more and more effort for less and less result. I was turning into a total slug.

Another problem I was having was with injuries. In my mid-fifties, I was finding that many times during my home workout, I would hurt my neck, or my back, or something, and this was concerning to me. I had already badly injured my neck while hanging some wallpaper, and that was really causing me pain. I had been to physical therapy for this neck issue (which incidentally, ran down the nerves into my right arm) and it had helped a lot. But it was still very easy to re-injure. I needed to be cautious.

My sister had been using a personal trainer for a number of years and seemed to like it. That idea had entered my mind a few times, but I never really thought about it seriously. My sister called her trainer her "personal torturer," and I should have taken that as a warning, but I thought she was just trying to be funny.

So, I decided to hire a personal trainer to at least get me on the right track with a personalized exercise program. I found one online that seemed like a good fit. He had lots of certifications. He said that he worked with all ages and was accustomed to working with people who had injuries and limitations.

Ok, perfect. I made an appointment.

At first it was awkward. He was a lot younger than me, and we didn't have a lot to talk about. But he was very focused and very conscious of my injuries, and he seemed to really have a desire to help me get stronger and healthier without hurting myself.

Great. *This isn't so bad*, I thought. *I can deal with this.*

As time progressed, we found more to talk about and the sessions went by pretty quickly. I started to look forward to the workouts, especially when COVID-19 hit and we had the lockdown. We continued to work out via Zoom during the shutdown. For me, it was nice just to have someone to interact with, and, since he had lost lots of clients due to gym-closures, he was happy to still have me.

He even tried to help me with my diet during that time and offered me some tips on how to make healthy meals. He was really big on Crock-pot usage. He would constantly tell me about all the easy meals I could make in a Crock-pot with little effort. I really didn't want to hear about the benefits of the slow cooker, but after a while he began to wear me down.

After COVID let up, we went back to meeting in person and things got back to normal. He even offered to prep some healthy meals for me and bring them ready to go in my Crock-pot. *That seems quite nice*, I thought.

But I was getting burnt out again.

I tried to fight it. I tried to act excited about my workouts. I even tried to act interested in the recipes he would bring up. I tried the slow cooker for a while. He was right. It was pretty easy and quite tasty. I used his recipes for the winter months.

But by spring, I quit cooking. I had used the Crock-pot to make healthy stews and soups until I wanted to toss it over the balcony—through his car windshield.

And this feeling of resentment, or something like that,

was growing.

I would literally count the minutes till Ricco got there. Not in the good way.

It was like, *oh crap, I only have fifteen minutes until he gets here. I need to change into my workout clothes. Damn. Ok, I'll just wait a couple more minutes.*

Then I'd think, *maybe just a couple more minutes. Maybe he will be late… I hope he's late. Or better yet, maybe he will have car trouble and have to cancel. Yes. Car trouble. Please God.*

As more time passed it got worse.

I could feel the hatred forming deep in my soul. I didn't want to feel that way. I just didn't think Ricco understood my complete disgust for working out or my need for more appreciation from him.

See, in the beginning, he would be so encouraging. He would comment on the progress I was making. He would throw out little compliments like "Good job!" and "Nice work!" after I had run up and down my stairs about twenty times — carrying twenty-pound weights in each hand — and was delirious and seeing stars.

I had no idea anyone could find so many ways to inflict pain on me in my own home, using furniture I once enjoyed. I now understood why my sister called her trainer her "personal torturer."

As more time passed, I felt like the honeymoon was over. He seemed to just expect me to work-out without any praise. I needed encouragement. I wanted some magic. I wanted him to give me energy. Possibly inject it — like an IV.

What I did *not* want was for him to point out that my

food choices were a large part of my energy problems.

He didn't seem to appreciate the dietary sacrifices I was making. I was using *whole wheat* bread for God's sake. I was drinking only water and unsweet tea, and no sodas—ever. Wasn't that enough? I didn't eat anything fried either. Not that I had in the twenty years before I met him, but I still wanted credit.

I did not like it when he said things like, "If you want to lose weight, you really can't eat two desserts every day." He literally wanted me to cut down to *one* desert a day and suggested that on *some* days I might skip desserts all together. The very idea. This was getting on my nerves, bad.

Oh, and he loved to rub it in, in subtle ways, that I was a slacker. I'd say something like, "What are you doing the rest of the day?"

And he'd say, "I have two more clients and then I'm going to run ten miles followed by my meal prep for the rest of the week."

Of course, I knew what he really meant: "I'm going to be working hard while you lay on your lazy ass the rest of the day."

Oh, and I never felt that he gave me adequate credit for being thirty-two years older than him. "Thirty-two years takes a toll on a body," I would tell him. But he would just say something encouraging like, "That's why it's so important to keep moving."

I began to hate him. I began to hate the sound of his car in the driveway. I hated to hear him knock on the door. It was a happy knock. Optimistic, like I was in for something fun, but I knew I wasn't.

I didn't want to hear that knock. I didn't want to hear

him say, "Hi" or hear him walk up the stairs to my little home workout area. I didn't like his little tight workout clothes that showed off his muscles either. Was I supposed to look like that? He looked like he had washed-up on a beach somewhere on some island, all tan and muscled. I knew I never would look like that.

I hated his name. Ricco. Sounded too cool. Like he was a trainer to the stars. Pain. Pain is what the name Ricco sounded like to me.

I dreamed of him taking long vacations. *Maybe he will move away*, I mused. *Yes, that's it. Maybe he will move and my torture would end.*

I hated him so much. It was palpable.

He never moved.

I finally fessed up to him. I told him that I dreamed of him missing appointments. I told him that I spent the hour before every session talking myself out of calling him and cancelling my workout. I would think, *I'll just tell him I'm sick*, but I feared karma. I feared a severe case of COVID-style karma. So I never made those cancellation calls. I continued to work out.

In response to my burn-out confession, he said he would re-write my workout plan.

Hmmm.

Was this a trick? Did I have a workout plan? I just thought that he was basically doing the same thing with everyone. But no, he said I had one, and that he would give me a new one to make things more interesting.

Well, shit. This was a plot twist.

"More interesting" turned out to be the exact same

thing as *more painful*.

I felt as if the new workout plan had been *inflicted on me* rather than *developed for me*. All the new exercises were making me sore in all kinds of new places. But I wasn't bored. I will give him that.

I wanted to ban him from my house—never see him again. I wanted to turn the little workout area in my condo back into the cute writing space it had been. I wanted to.

But I knew I could not.

I knew what awaited me. I knew that as much as I dreaded him walking up the steps of my condo, I would also hate to feel the way I felt *before* I began working out with Ricco. I knew that slowly—actually quickly—I would morph back into the slug I had become when I quit the gym. I also knew that I was not going to rejoin the gym or pick up yoga again—like I would often try to convince myself.

I knew that Ricco was my only hope for any kind of regular workouts. The accountability was something I needed, and having an appointment to workout seemed to be the only way I could force myself. I hated to admit it just as much as I hated him.

I really do hate him.

Really, I do.

So much.

NOT THE BIRD...AGAIN

Birds love me. At least that's what it feels like. They seem to want to be as close to me as possible. They build nests on my terrace, right outside my window. It gets irritating, but I tolerate it.

Actually, if you really observe them, they just prove that we, as humans, are complete slackers.

It all started several years back, at my old condo. My bedroom had a closet right by my bed that housed the air conditioning unit. The unit itself was noisy, but I had learned to sleep through that. What I could not sleep through was the nest of baby birds screaming at the top of their lungs, demanding to be fed at five a.m.

This air conditioning unit sat in an opening in the wall that went to the terrace. The opening was covered by louvers, but the louver at the bottom was big enough for a bird to get through. So, when the bird came in through the louver, into the air conditioning unit, it was actually sitting inside the closet, right by my bed.

I wanted to get the nest out and remove the birds, but I knew that the mama bird would never touch them again. I feared I would be carrying around a nest of screeching birds with an eye dropper full of sugar water for the next several weeks.

So, I waited them out.

I don't stay in Nashville every day of the week, so at least I could sleep when I was not there. But when I was there, managing my new fly-in Air B&B, it was miserable. I could not believe how often that bird was feeding those chirping babies. She was in a constant flight pattern to and from the nest in my unit. I was anxiously waiting for the day they would take their first flights so I could remove the nest and regain my regular sleeping pattern.

Then one day I found a little bird casualty lying on my terrace floor. I guess the rest of them survived their first attempt at flight. Finally, the chirping went silent and I could sleep.

It took some doing to get the intricately built nest out of its cavern, but I did, and then cleaned up all the mess. I decided to put some gray duct tape over the gap in the louvers so that I would not have to worry about the noise again. Duct tape is really sticky and pretty weather resistant, so I figured that would take care of the problem.

Wrong.

A month or so later, I noticed that the duct tape had been peeled back from the metal louver. And then I saw a bird, I supposed a different one, busily finishing up a nest. I was furious.

I was also amazed.

I tried peeling back the rest of the duct tape and I felt a good bit of resistance from the remaining tape. I had a hard time getting it off. How on earth did that bird do it? And why was this such a desirable location for a nest? Was there some sort of bulletin board that the birds checked to get recommendations for nest locations? I was imagining the ad that was posted by my first bird.

"Nice nest available, recently vacated on the eighth floor of a modern high-rise in midtown. Noise from the big fan kicking on and off can be jarring, but no wind or rain issues. Cool temperatures even on hot days. Difficult for snakes to get to and is relatively safe, except for this giant human who keeps looking through the vent opening. He also occasionally screams at us to shut our beaks, but overall, much better than tree residences."

I really wanted to get a look at this new bird. She must have been at the aviary gym every day, pumping up her little wings to get ready. I couldn't imagine how she got that tape off the opening and why she just didn't seek out another unit. Somehow, she was able to grab that duct tape with her beak (I suppose) and flap those little wings fast enough to generate the strength to pull it back.

I guess the new mama was very disappointed when she could not find the used nest in my air conditioning unit, but she was not discouraged. She proceeded to build a new one. I thought about throwing out the new nest she was building, but I was worried that the bird wouldn't have time to build another one somewhere else.

So, I braced myself for the eventual screaming.

Being in the construction business, I couldn't help but think about the planning skills and stamina this poor little mama bird must have. In my business, building a house—even a simple one—is at least a six-month project involving multiple crews of workers and equipment and deliveries and inspections. This bird could scope out a building site, prep it, bring in the materials needed, weave them into a safe and secure structure, all while carrying the eggs. I'm not sure if the male birds help any with the nest construction, but in this case, I never saw one. I do think they help with the feeding, but that's kind of like a man saying, "I'll stop by Walgreens and pick up some formula," after his wife has built the house single-handedly and given birth.

I have to give props to ants too. I've seen a couple of them move a Cheerio across a kitchen floor. Yes, Cheerios are not that heavy to humans. But to an ant? I would say otherwise. I'd roughly equate it to seeing me and a friend carrying a Buick sedan around on our backs for the afternoon.

The speed at which a spider can weave an intricate web is another one of nature's wonders. It always infuriates me when I walk into one and get the sticky web in my hair and on my clothes, but then I'll go back to the same place the next day and there will be a newly constructed web, right there in the same place.

Amazing.

I can't say as much for the squirrels though.

I think they may be watching us humans a bit too much—me in particular—and have become lazy. I have some furniture on my patio with cushions and throw pillows that I don't use very much, but in the last couple of years, when I've moved a throw pillow, I have discovered a hidden walnut. This has happened many times. I thought squirrels buried their nuts, but not so at my house. My squirrels are just plain lazy. Sticking a nut under a throw pillow sure isn't doing much to secure it for the winter. But I don't like digging in the yard either, so maybe we are kindred spirits.

After the second bird built her nest in my air conditioning unit, and after a couple of weeks of the screaming for food coming from her little family, I decided I was through with the birds. When they were finally gone, I screwed a piece of metal over the opening and ended my bird hatchery. This proved to be very effective and I never saw another nest at that condo.

A year or two later, though, I moved out of that condo and into another one around the corner. Then we had a year of COVID isolation. In the second spring of COVID, I discovered that the birds had found me again. This time I discovered an ingenious little nest in the pot of ivy I keep on the balcony off my bedroom. Are birds just attracted to me? Do they like to watch me sleep? Because once again they chose to locate very close to my bed.

This nest was built more like a cave, with a roof. I looked online and identified it as a wren's nest. At least that's the closest thing I could find. My balcony is covered and shady, so I could see the attraction. Then I saw the tiny whitish eggs—four or five of them. I didn't want to get too close and scare her, but I did still have to water my ivy. I looked a couple of times and saw no baby birds. The mama would come and go, but no chirping.

I was kind of excited about the new lives. The loss of life brought about by COVID-19 had me anxious to see any kind of rebirth. It's always been amazing to me— nature and what happens while we aren't paying attention. But I began to really worry about this little wren and how she was going to feed five babies. I put out a pan of water so she could stay hydrated—lord knows, I didn't want to have to provide assistance with the feeding process.

I also bought some little tins of moist dog food. According to my online sources, this is good to leave out to feed birds. Seems illogical, I know. But I wanted that mama bird to have plenty of fuel so she could make all those necessary flights to feed those little chirping chicks. My thinking was that if she were well fed, she could keep them quiet.

I didn't put out the dog food though, because I got to thinking that other animals might smell it and come and eat the eggs, thus making the entire thing rather counterproductive. I thought I would wait until the birds hatched and I could see the mama bird in action. Then I'd put out the food, but remove it as soon as she ate. I left the water out all the time.

After a few more days though, I noticed the bird had quit coming to check on the nest. I was hoping she was just sitting in the nest with her eggs, but I took a look and she was nowhere to be found. I kept watching for her to return and still no mama bird. I was really beginning to worry that I was going to have to raise five baby birds. I really didn't think I had that skill set.

I looked on the internet again and found out how long it took for the eggs to hatch and noted that these eggs were overdue—by several days. Sadly, they never hatched. I guess the mama knew they were not going to hatch and abandoned them. We had had a couple of cool nights during this period and I thought maybe that was it, but I really didn't know.

I had tried to keep my distance from them. I tried to be a good foster dad, and even tried to be a supportive spouse to my little wren mama, stocking up on supplies and all.

But alas, no baby birds.

No chirping at five a.m.

And as much as I hated to admit it, I missed them.

A CRUISE? I'LL TAKE MINE NUDE

Some of my friends asked me to go along on a Caribbean cruise. I had heard them talk in glowing terms about some of the cruises they had been on in the past. I was pretty sure I would *not* enjoy it.

The Caribbean part concerned me. My friends were all sun lovers and I was not. I am pale and burn easily. The thought of lying on a deck chair for hours —or even minutes—baking in the sun had no appeal to me. They assured me that there would be plenty of other things to do and that there were shady spots all over the ship. I had never thought I would be a cruise person, but I love to travel and I thought maybe I needed to find out. With some reservations, no pun intended, I decided to tag along.

At dinner, I wasn't thrilled about sitting with strangers, but that seemed to be the way you do things on a cruise. So when our group of four was seated with another group of four, I tried to act like I was happy to meet them. At first glance they looked like just your average middle-aged couples. I was very wrong.

Brian and Robin were the younger of the two couples, and they were probably in their mid-forties. The other couple, Tom and Susan, were probably in their late fifties. All of them had a clean-cut appearance, nothing remarkable about them.

But I could tell, even in the early stages of the conversation, that they were *fishing*.

I wasn't sure what they were fishing for—maybe our political leanings or maybe our religion, I didn't know—but, for sure, they were sizing us up. Then, after more chatting, it occurred to me that their interest was lifestyle related. It didn't take long for them to get to the heart of the matter.

They were nudists. And proud of it.

According to Brian, who seemed to be the spokesman for the group, the reason they were on this very cruise was because of their nude lifestyle.

We were a bit shocked, and asked if there was something about the cruise we were currently on that we needed to know. Perhaps we had missed a paragraph in the brochure mentioning a "clothing optional" part of the ship, or maybe there was a "nude evening" we knew nothing about. I knew one thing for certain, I was not about to be getting buck naked in front of my new friends—or the old ones either for that matter.

He assured us that we had not missed anything and there was nothing nude going on during our current cruise. However, he explained, the reason they were on this particular ship was because the *next* cruise on this ship would indeed be a *nude cruise.*

Brian took great pride in telling us that next week the entire ship would be full of completely nude passengers. Over three thousand bare butts strolling the upper and lower decks for all to see. Our group was pretty gob-smacked by this little bit of intel.

None of us had ever heard of a nude cruise.

Brian and Tom said that there were several nude cruises every year on various major cruise lines, and they all sold out a year in advance. They said we should go right to this nude-cruise website and look into booking a future cruise. Tom said, "They really fill up fast, but you might find some cancellations for one this year." Apparently, the fact that we were asking some questions about the cruises indicated that we might be interested in a trip.

We still didn't understand why they were on the ship with us, seeing that we were on a *clothing-required* cruise. Brian went on to explain that they were from Connecticut, and he had two weeks of vacation. So they booked two cruises back-to-back, on the same ship. This way, they could just stay on the ship and keep the same room for the nude cruise the following week. Of course, in Brian's perfect world, both cruises would be nude, but they just had to settle for what they could get. And being in the sun, away from the bitter New England mid-January winter, in a very skimpy speedo was better than nothing.

My friends and I were still having a very hard time believing all of this. They were all pretty avid cruisers and they had not heard of nude cruises. But Brian and Robin were so full of details, they had us convinced it was a real thing. I even asked one of the staff members if it were true and he—with a roll of his eyes—said, "Oh yes, it's very true. We have been in training for a couple of weeks."

"Training?" I said.

"Yes," Albert said. Albert was our head steward, in charge of our dinner service for the cruise and had already introduced himself to us.

"What kind of training?" I said. Curiosity was killing me.

"You know, proper eye contact, where to look and not to look, and additional sanitation requirements. That kind of thing."

"Ahh." I said. I was thinking that sounded really disgusting, but I tried not to show it. "Have you worked one of these before?"

"No, but I have heard about them," Albert said with a slight eye-roll meant just for me.

Brian reclaimed the conversation and went into great detail about all the pros of a nude cruise. The sense of freedom seemed to be the main one. Another big advantage was the ease of packing. "It's a breeze!" he said.

Robin said, with a frown, that even on the nude cruise they were required to *dress* for dinner. But, she said, "I just wear something light and sheer, so I don't feel confined." I couldn't help but look over at Albert and wonder if he liked the thought of that. Albert's income was largely subsidized by tips, though, and he remained pretty neutral and expressionless.

Because we all were asking questions about the nude cruise, I guess Tom, Brian and Robin felt that we were really interested in taking one. Trust me on this, they had completely misinterpreted the situation. None of us had any interest whatsoever. But we did find it all quite fascinating. I do love talking to off-beat folks and these guys were right down my alley.

On the subsequent nights, Brian went into great detail about all the fun events that would be taking place on the nude cruise. He said they had theme nights every night and that dressing for those was a lot of fun. Again, I just had to ask: "What kind of dressing?"

Robin said that for Mardi Gras night they had packed some beads to wear. *Of course*, I thought. Then for the formal night Brian had packed a bow-tie and Robin her diamond earrings. Tom kind of kept quiet, like he had some surprises up his sleeve. (But then I thought, *No, that's wrong, he won't have any sleeves*.) The last night would be a masquerade ball and my assumption was correct. They would all wear masks and nothing else. Maybe some heels for Robin.

Susan, Tom's wife, was always quiet. Tom was quite talkative and really into all the nudist conversation, but Susan was reserved. I got the idea that she might not be totally into nudism, but then again, maybe she was just quiet. She didn't even tell us about her costumes, so we just had to wonder what she might wear, but, really, the options were limited.

The first stop on our trip was Key West. All during dinner the night before we arrived, Brian and Tom assured us that just because we were not on the nude cruise with them *next* week, we could still "get nude" with them on this cruise.

They explained that there was a bar in Key West that was clothing optional, and they planned to go there as soon as the ship docked and spend the day nude. Tom said, "You guys really should come. The four of us will be there all day. Nude. There are others on this cruise that are nudists too, and you can meet them as well."

Shockingly, not one of my group of friends took them up on the offer. None of us had been to Key West before, so we had planned to sight-see. (But if we had already seen all the Key West sights, well, who knows?) Robin and Brian expressed their disappointment and continued to urge us to reconsider. "There just aren't that many bars you can visit and spend the day nude," they said. But we held firm.

I hadn't told any of my friends, but after our first conversation with the nudists, I had gone to the website they mentioned and done a bit of investigating. It was all true. There were two or three all-nude cruises a year on alternating major cruise lines. According to the photos, they were filled with beautiful young men and women in their twenties or thirties with perfectly tanned and toned bodies, lying about the deck in seductive positions. As I was looking at this, it occurred to me that our table-mates did not look like the people pictured on the website. So, I did a little more investigating.

Online, I found that the average age of most of the nude-cruisers was around sixty-five. So obviously, the photographer for the website had been there on a "good day." So, now, the scene I was picturing in my head was a ship full of senior citizens, walking around nude with bow-ties and diamond earrings. It took me a little while to shake that image.

My research proved to be true. Over the course of the week, we would run into Tom or Robin on the ship and they would introduce us to some other nudists that were also doing the nude cruise the following week. Almost all of them were in their sixties or seventies. Not that there is anything wrong with that. More power to them I say, and good for you if that makes you happy. But I really didn't want to see Uncle Bob and Aunt Sally wearing just their sagging skin and a pair of sunglasses. Call me a prude.

Now, I'm guessing that nudists might argue that I have missed the whole point of the lifestyle. I'm guessing they would say they just enjoy the freedom of being nude and, after a while, they don't even notice the other nude bodies. You just look right past your friend's large or small attributes, right into their soul.

Maybe that is all true. But then I wonder why the website isn't full of photos of the real *average* nudists. Obviously, they are using the oldest advertising ploy in the book—young beautiful people—to attract attention.

At every island stop on our week-long trip, we were urged to go with our new friends to a nude beach or a nude hangout. They had definitely done their homework. If there was a place within ten miles where you could legally drop-trousers in public, they knew all about it. They were obsessed. We respectfully declined each time, and one would think they would have gotten the hint. But they all said that if we did it just once, we would be hooked.

One night, Tom and Susan were absent at dinner. I could tell that Brian and Robin had more going on than just nudism, and this gave them a good chance to let us in on some things. It was obvious they had been holding back all week, even after their nude lifestyle had become known.

By this time, they felt comfortable with my group of friends, so they told us that not only were they nudists —they were also both bi-sexual swingers. I wasn't really surprised, they just had that look about them. You could just tell they were an up-for-anything type couple. And I think their being bi-sexual nudist swingers pretty much covered any possible situation that might arise.

Oh, did I forget to mention the rules? Yeah, they said they did have one rule. They could swing with anyone, just as long as the other partner was always present. The more I thought about it, I couldn't imagine any situation, orientation, or lifestyle that Robin and Brian could not participate in—together of course. Straight couples, gay couples, singles—well, virtually anyone was fair game for the two of them.

After dinner, we all tried to figure out if there was some sort of invitation in that disclosure, but none of us could pin down what it might be, or who they might want it to be with, so we decided not to bring that up again. Honestly, though, I could not wait to get home and tell my other friends that I had been having dinner every night with bi-sexual nudist swingers. It had such a great ring to it.

Near the end of the cruise—maybe it was our last night dining with our new nude friends, I'm not sure— Albert (maybe having overheard our week-long conversation about nudity) told us to look out the window at the little island in the distance.

It was a small island, maybe a mile wide, hard to tell.

Albert said that it was called the "naked island" because clothing wasn't required anywhere on the island.

"Really?" Brian said.

"Not even at dinner?" Robin said.

Our friends rushed to the window, eyes watering and

mouths salivating. Right there, in the distance, was their utopia.

It was kind of sad, though, knowing how bad they wanted to be let off the ship there on the island and disrobe. I could tell Robin was thinking about eating all her meals nude and not even having to dress for dinner. The freedom of it. They couldn't stop staring at that tiny island of their dreams.

After the island blurred in the distance, they returned to the table, bleary-eyed and dejected, but at the same time hopeful they might someday get to visit. Dinner conversation returned to normal. They told us how much they would miss us and, once again, urged us to consider a nude cruise. "We should all book one together," Brian urged. "Then we could attend all the fun events together!"

My friends and I had to give them credit. They didn't give up easily.

I've been on cruises since that one. But I must say, that first one stands out in my memory. On the next cruise, I got what I expected as dining companions; a dentist and his wife, an advertising agent—the usual types. We had a few laughs, and they were nice. We heard about their kids and their travels.

But it was all pretty dull really—not once did they ask us to take off our clothes.

MONKEY BUSINESS

I was incredibly frustrated when I found out. How could I have been so unlucky and missed this? But I did.

The manager at our business had put out word that he was looking to hire a replacement for an employee that had quit. Nothing new. People come in everyday to fill out job applications.

So, a man comes in, with his wife, and with a monkey on his shoulder, in a diaper. Not the man, the monkey was in the diaper.

The man asked my manager about the job and then asked to fill out an application. The wife said to the husband, "I'll hold the baby," while he filled out the application.

When I got back to the office and found out about this, I asked a thousand questions.

But my manager did not get *nearly* enough information to satisfy me.

I must admit, I've always been a little bit fascinated by monkeys. I kind of wanted one as a pet for a while, but thought better of it.

I really wanted to know if the "baby" was literally a

baby, and if that was why it was wearing a diaper, or if it was an adult monkey and just wore a diaper all the time.

I also wanted to get inside the mind of a man who would bring along a monkey to apply for a job.

Why didn't the wife and the baby just stay in the car?

Did the man think the monkey would help him secure the position? *That's a serious roll of the dice*, I thought.

Some employers might be completely turned off at the prospect of adding a monkey as a dependent to the company health insurance plan. But others, like me, might be truly fascinated by it.

According to my manager, the man didn't have the experience we needed for the job. But I still wanted to call him in for an interview.

I wondered if he would bring the monkey and his wife along to the interview? I wondered, if he was hired, was he planning to bring the baby along to work every day? The curiosity was eating away at me.

Couldn't we just bring him in for the interview?

But the other side of it is that I truly hate to waste anyone's time, and I knew it would be really selfish of me to call him in for an interview knowing that I probably wouldn't hire him. And I certainly wouldn't want him to miss out on another opportunity while I had him in my office drilling him with questions about the monkey, and what he (the monkey) did all day, and where one would go to find monkey diapers.

Damn. I was torn.

I didn't call him in. Even though I really, really wanted to.

I just marked it down as an odd office occurrence that I, sadly, missed.

Being in the office is never dull. I mean, every day isn't as exciting as the whole monkey thing, but the people I work with are all genuinely funny. We like to keep the mood light.

There is this one *situation*, you might call it, that has been discussed around the office for a long time—I'm talking at least a couple of years. I'm going to have to put it in the category of *odd-things*, along with the monkey.

One day, it is a Teenage Mutant Ninja Turtle, another day it is Mickey Mouse.

I'm talking about the costumed person down the street from my office. They are standing out in front of their business, every day—rain or shine, sleet or snow.

Every day.

Every single day.

The dedication of these costume-wearers is epic. Yesterday, in the snow and freezing temps, one of them was out, all day long, fully costumed and waving at the cars as they drove by. I have seen them out all-day on scorching-hot summer days as well. Minnie, or Mickey, or somebody is there every weekday. I pass by multiple times a day, going back and forth to work and to jobs and such. I cannot tell you about Saturday or Sunday because I am always in Nashville, but I have heard they are out on those days too. They are fully committed.

I also can't tell you the name of the business; the sign is much too small to read. It's only about three feet wide and printed in pastel colors. You can't read it from a distance, and it's even hard to make out up-close. The building has no display windows like a typical store would, so you can't see in.

After about a year of the costumed-characters standing out front, my friend Maggie finally got curious enough to stop by. This is exactly what they wanted, I feel sure. Maggie is the first person (that I know of) that actually stopped there, so I would say the marketing plan obviously has sort of a slow burn.

Maggie found out upon entering the store that it is a catalog liquidation place. We have several of those in town. (I have been known to frequent some of them because sometimes you can find some cool stuff.) Maggie, being the good citizen that she is, tried hard to find something to buy. I think she ended up with a Rubbermaid garbage can, but don't hold me to that.

She also, in a kind way, told the owner that she might want to put up a larger sign or do *something* to let passersby know what was in the shop. Maggie wasn't sure if the owner appreciated her advice, so she went on her way. Before Maggie left, she did find out that the owner had previously owned a costume shop, which did explain a lot. Maggie also learned that it was the owner's children out front in the costumes. The owner said they just loved dressing-up and standing out front.

We wondered why she didn't let the costumed children hold a sign pointing toward the store, explaining what was inside. But when I thought more about it, the answer was really so obvious: that would have been totally *out of character*.

A while later though, Maggie and I noticed that

someone had put some of the merchandise outside on the front sidewalk, where it could be seen. At least this did give people some idea of what might be inside. I'm not sure the choice of merchandise really made sense, though.

Last week for example, Moana (I think she is a Disney Princess) was out front waving at folks, and there was a potty-chair on display right behind her.

In fact there has been a potty-chair out front for several months now. There was also a piece of exercise equipment, some walking canes in a bin, and a large piece of art.

Occasionally, the items on display do change, but not nearly as frequently as when they first began putting the items outside.

The costumes, however, change daily and you never know who is going to be waving to you. Recently, I've seen Minions, Buzz Lightyear, a Teletubby, and a variety of others. They always wear the full costume, complete with the headpiece.

I have been driving by the place for a good two years, multiple times a day, and I can say this without hesitation: I have *never, ever* seen a customer going into or leaving the store. I've even polled my friends and co-workers as well, and none of them have seen any customers there either. We've spent a good deal of time talking about this over the years. Once, I saw someone stop to get photos of Mickey Mouse with their children, and they *might* have gone in, but I don't know for sure.

Curiosity got the best of me one day, and I stopped in.

I was surprised how small it was. I think most of the space must be consumed with costume storage. They had a lot of the basic catalog return stuff, but also a few things I wasn't expecting. They had a big display of sports bras and another big table full of socks. They looked like good quality socks. There were some lamps, some chairs (none matching), a few odd tables, maybe some baskets as I recall, and a table with a lot of knee-high hose.

It would never occur to me, when driving by a Teenage Mutant Ninja Turtle to think, *Oh, I bet they have sports bras.* If I owned that store, I would be tempted to, at the very least, put Minnie Mouse out front in one of the many sports bras to see if it brought in any new customers.

So far, they have not.

During the times I *don't* pass by there, I suppose they could be flooded with customers. They might be selling so much merchandise they simply can't find the time to change the outdoor display.

And who knows how many incontinent persons might have been lured in after viewing the potty chair out front? They might also be making tons of sales online. Maybe they have become known for their selection of sports bras on the web.

I have thought about this more than I would like to admit.

Who am I to judge their marketing strategy anyway? What do I know?

I'm sure that kids passing by on their way to school or to Wal-mart love seeing the characters each day.

The store owners could be doing all of it as a community service and, if so, props to them.

I always wave at the characters when I pass by.

(They started it, so I am just being cordial.)

I do think the kids are getting tired though. I know I would be—standing out there every day in the wind and the rain and the cold.

I'm also keeping my eye-out for the man and his monkey as I drive around town. I told my manager to call me immediately if he happens to come back in, even interrupt me in an important meeting if need be. I want to interview him. I have so many questions.

Maybe by then a suitable position within the company will have opened up.

NASHVILLE IS IT!

At first, it seemed like a cool thing: living in an "it" city, a city everyone suddenly wanted to visit, a city everyone wanted to move to.

The new wore off quickly, though. Very quickly.

Now I'd like to tag another city and say, "You're it!" Let Omaha or Dubuque have some of the fun for a while.

It all started off gradually. First, Nashville got a professional hockey team. This seemed like an odd fit to me, but it really caught on. Then pro football came to town and really ramped-up things with a new stadium downtown by the river. I'm no sports fan, but at least it cleaned up a dirty industrial area and spurred development along the river. *That's cool*, I thought.

When I first started visiting Nashville in the 1980s, downtown was pretty much dead. There were a few bars frequented by the die-hard country music enthusiasts, only a few nice restaurants and hotels, and a lot of government buildings. On Third Avenue there was a big architectural salvage company—the first one I had ever visited. Then south of Broadway there were the fabric and rug stores that I loved and frequented. Some of the downtown churches were still active as well.

But the downtown movie theaters had been closed for years, and all of them had been torn down. Down on Lower Broadway there was a good bit of adult-themed entertainment and peep shows, and there were lots of empty buildings.

When I thought about getting a place in Nashville, I didn't want to live downtown. Although lofts were beginning to be developed on a lot of the upper floors of the old buildings, it wasn't a place I felt I could walk safely at night. And I definitely wanted to be in a walkable area.

I decided to locate in midtown, near Vanderbilt campus, in a tiny one-bedroom condo. I would only be there on the weekends, so I didn't need a lot of space. There were lots of places to eat close-by and beautiful areas to walk on the nearby college campuses. I even joined the downtown YMCA since I was only a few blocks from downtown. I loved the new downtown public library—they had a great selection of recorded books. I also enjoyed seeing shows at the Ryman Auditorium, the Tennessee Performing Arts Center, and the new Arena.

As I began to spend more time in Nashville—and after ten years in the little condo—I decided to upgrade to a larger place in the same building. I had grown to love the location, right in the middle of everything. So when I heard that Marshall Chapman's two-bedroom unit on the eighth floor was available, I had to take a look. I made the mistake of going up there at night and the views were spectacular. It had panoramic views of the city. I was sold. I made an offer the next day.

I knew that Marshall was a popular Nashville singer/songwriter, but I didn't know that she called her condo the "Sky Palace", or that she had written about it in a song. She used to have many famous friends over for songwriting sessions. At the closing, she told me that Emmylou Harris, Matraca Berg and Kris Kristofferson, among others, would visit and write with her there. I also found out that she used the profits from her number one song, *Betty's Being Bad* to pay for the Sky Palace.

All of this is in her book, *Goodbye Little Rock and Roller.* I highly recommend it. She is an authentic Nashville character. She has done it all, worked with many master musicians, and her biography is a wild ride. A lot of it occurred in my new place. I must admit, I had never listened to any of her music before reading her book, but after I did, I became a big fan. The book is true singer/songwriter storytelling, and she does it well.

Before she sold the place to me, she rented it for a few years to Mario, of the locally famous Mario's Italian Restaurant.

I wondered if I was a letdown to my new condo after it had housed two such well-known Nashville characters. Marshall had told me at the closing that the condo had good vibes and that, since it was on the top floor, those good vibes would flow right in through the ceiling. I have to agree. I loved living there.

When I first moved in though, I was having problems with air-conditioning in the second bathroom. I noticed that the vent was blocked and, upon removing the vent cover, I found a couple of large suit bags filled with something squishy. It sort of freaked me out.

The first thing that ran through my mind was that I had found the remains of Janet March. You may recall the famous Nashville murder case. She went missing, and her husband Perry was always suspected. But they never could find the body. The search went on for years and the case garnered nationwide interest before Perry was finally convicted in 2006.

Well, right before I moved into the building, I heard from the security guard that Perry March had rented a unit there for a year or two, after Janet went missing. The security guard even told me that the police had searched the building looking for evidence. I didn't know what unit he had rented. For all I knew, it could have been mine. Maybe he rented it before Mario moved in? Or, maybe he snuck in and put the body there?

It took me a few minutes to decide to go ahead and open the suit bags. Thankfully, they were just full of old blankets and some of Mario's old clothes. I used to see him on the elevator and they seemed to be his type of apparel. So I decided to close the case. I was very relieved.

Every time I went to the gym, or the library, or a concert, though, I would notice a bit more of what was being termed as "progress": either an old building coming down, or a new building going up, as well as more and more traffic. The changes were happening fast. Progress was closing in all around me.

I had loved to watch the Fourth-of-July fireworks from my balcony. Over the years the displays got bigger and bigger and then, suddenly, Nashville was the go-to destination for the Fourth. At first, I could see the entire display without any obstruction. But by the year I moved out of that building, I could only see a few whiffs of smoke rising above all the new downtown hotels. The bigger the display got over the years, the less of it I could see.

What had brought me to this building was now gone. I was ready to move away from so much traffic and noise. I hated to leave that condo. But I didn't move far. I'm still in the middle of everything, but just far enough away to avoid a lot of the tourists and most of the noise.

All of this progress began to really make me feel very nostalgic. It's not that I am anti-progress. I do, however, miss a lot of things, like all the old buildings in my Nashville neighborhood.

I embrace modern architecture. I like a lot of it very much. I just don't like it when a gorgeous old home, or an apartment building with beautiful architectural detail, is bulldozed in order to build a modern one.

Recently, I've been thinking about an old *The Andy Griffith Show* episode. It's the one where the gang was sitting on Andy's front porch reminiscing about the good old days, wishing they still had Sunday afternoon band concerts in the park. So they decide to bring them back. They all exhaust themselves trying to repair the bandstand and get the band back in practice. But by the end of the episode, they realize the moment has passed.

Of course, if Andy's cute little home was in Nashville, it would have already been torn down and two tall-and-skinny houses would be built in its place. Big, friendly front porches are becoming as scarce as neighbors who would actually drop by to sit on them.

There isn't any question in my mind that the moment has passed in Nashville. Nashville has officially transitioned. The old, slower-paced Nashville with mostly life-long residents is gone. Nashville is a train speeding down a track, heading straight toward traffic congestion and overcrowding. Actually, we have already arrived at the station.

I could see it all unfolding as I walked the track at the downtown YMCA. I would look out the windows and see the construction cranes dotting the skyline. So many cranes it was often hard to keep count. They were everywhere.

Downtown is now filled with trendy new restaurants, hotels and bars. Lots and lots of bars—or "honkytonks", I should say. And they are all filled with tourists. Droves and droves of them. People spill out of the bars onto the sidewalks and streets, and now traffic is either at a standstill or cut off completely.

The tourist area has expanded from Second and Third Avenues to a multi-block radius of that old downtown core. Music, of course, is what Nashville has always been known for, but the downtown now seems to have taken on a life of its own as a party mecca. Someone said recently that it was like New Orleans and Las Vegas had sex in a field and their love-child was Nashville. I think that's pretty accurate.

The good thing about the tourists is that they are easy to spot—and hopefully avoid.

Nashville has become the number-one destination for bridal groups and most of them dress alike while they are in town. They still wear cut-off jean shorts with cowboy boots in the dead of summer.

This trend died everywhere else in the nineties, but these gals are trying to keep it alive. Funny thing is, they think it originated in Nashville, but no locals ever wore that. Nor do the locals wear cowboy hats or cowboy boots. The only locals you will see in those things are the ones about to step on a stage and perform a set of country music standards.

On their last night in town, the leader of the pack (the bride) will usually wear a white cowboy hat with a white veil hanging off the back so that she may be easily identified. I'm guessing that she is expecting some free deserts or drinks. I don't know if that works or not, but I do know that they seem to have a very good time.

The bride weekend trips are not complete without a ride around town on a pedal tavern—a way to get exercise and drink simultaneously. It's this little covered-wagon, with ten stools that all have pedals. Every person pedals to power the wagon, but they dispense beer from a keg to keep you energized. The other day on Music Row at the round-about (that's the one with the controversial nude statues), I was behind a trolley tavern. A bride was riding on the back seat, right in front of me, where she was affectionately holding a huge four-foot-long blow-up penis and yelling a lot of profane things out at cars passing by.

I couldn't help but think what a proud moment this will be for her parents when those pics make it onto all her social media accounts and her friends' accounts too. Then again, maybe I should be more concerned about what her groom thinks—talk about great expectations.

Nashville can now provide a vast array of choices when it comes to party transportation. The other day I was behind an all-glass party wagon that had a hot tub inside. There were about eight guys in the hot tub, drinking, and the rest were hanging-out over on the other side of the wagon where there was some additional seating and a toweling-off area. They seemed to be having a great time—hot-tubbing in traffic.

I have seen John Deere tractors pulling wagons full of hay bales with guests enjoying an old-fashioned hayride, and I have seen a very large bus that had a side removed and replaced with large glass panels. Inside there were three stripper-poles with a couple of strippers, at work, on said poles. I think there were some patrons inside the bus with them, but I am not really sure about the purpose of the glass wall. I suppose they are trying to share their good time with everyone else in traffic? Or maybe trying to drum-up business for the home office? Either way, I was not expecting strippers in traffic.

People visit Nashville, love it, and come back. They can't seem to get enough of it.

Many of them move here. The latest statistics report that about eighty-two people a day move to Nashville. That's almost thirty thousand people a year. The last time I checked, we don't have any new roads to accommodate their vehicles, but apartment complexes are being built at record pace to house them. I just looked it up, and Nashville is now number six on the "Top Party Cities in the USA" list. After New

Orleans, but ahead of Los Angeles. A proud moment indeed.

On the upside, the bridal groups now put even more thought into their visits. Many of them have matching outfits for each day, and if they don't, I consider them just plain lazy. The group I was sitting across from the other night at my little neighborhood Italian restaurant were all wearing neon-pink or neon-green wigs. I guess you had your choice based on your skin tone. They were hard to miss. And they were shockingly well-behaved—but it was pretty early in the evening.

I miss the old structures that made my neighborhood so cool when I first moved there: the mix of old houses and businesses. My favorite restaurants have, one by one, been converted into bars or forced out due to re-development. I miss these small local restaurants that weren't trendy or cliché—just good. That's all they needed to be. Now it seems they need a theme or a gimmick. A new restaurant just opened near me, and I was hoping for a good new seafood place. But nope, I was wrong. Their specialty you ask? Donuts. An entire restaurant dedicated to donuts.

A really tough pill to swallow was the closing of Brentwood Interiors. I heard they closed due to the rent increases that progress brings. It was my go-to store for fabric and rugs and other design needs.

I keep reminding myself that if I want to enjoy the *new* stores, the ones that have moved here because of our new demographics, I have to put up with the other stuff. Sure, it's nice to have a Crate and Barrel, but if I had my choice, I'd much rather have Brentwood

Interiors back open for business.

Still, there are many wonderful things about Nashville. The improvements to Centennial Park are just stunning. And people here remain as friendly as always.

So, I try not to focus on the extra time it takes to get anywhere since our roads are so much busier now.

I try not to notice the huge property tax increases.

I try not to notice the constant dodging of construction zones in my neighborhood.

I tell myself that the layer of black soot from all the construction that coats everything on my terrace is only a minor inconvenience. I try to take in some of the art exhibits, concerts, and other events that come our way, even if they do involve a trip to the congested downtown.

I keep thinking it will eventually begin to slow down.

I tell myself that, but I can't help but notice it actually seems to be picking up speed.

This is what happens in an "It" city, I am told. Old Nashville is forever gone. New Nashville is something yet undefined.

So here I am, in the middle of it, watching and wondering, nostalgic and adjusting—reluctantly a part of "it"—hoping another city will get tagged soon.

COFFEE CULTURE

I know millennials and Gen Yers will be repulsed—and feel sorry for my family—when I tell you what I am about to tell you. But it is all true, every disgusting word.

I grew up without coffee options. None.

We had Maxwell House and that's it. You had to put it in the percolator and brew it, and then drink it the rest of the day. There were no designer coffee shops in my town, just diners where you could get a cup of black coffee for about fifty cents, with all the free refills you wanted. Starbucks didn't exist. Well, at least not in the South.

And get ready, because now I am going to tell you something even worse.

It's bad.

Really bad.

But I'm going to go ahead and admit it right here. Sometimes when my mother was in a hurry and didn't have time to use the percolator to brew a pot of coffee, she made instant coffee.

Instant. There, I said it.

She just opened the Sanka jar and put a tablespoon of coffee grounds in a cup of hot water and bam: coffee.

It seemed to do the job, and Mom never complained. But today, I cannot image the looks I would get should I suggest such a thing to any of the Starbucks generation.

We had only one choice—no coffee grinder, no fresh ground, no dark blend or light blends. Just *coffee*. If you wanted something like a latte, you could add a little milk. If you asked for latte-foam art, the waitress would have drawn something in your cup with her cigarette.

To be honest, I don't drink coffee. Never have. I never tried a lot of the other options either. Once, in my twenties when I was in Italy, a friend had me try espresso. I thought it was horrible: tasted like syrup—and not the good kind you put on pancakes.

I have been to Starbucks, though, a few times. It's fascinating. When did such a simple thing become so complicated? Just the thought of ordering a coffee at Starbucks literally *gives* me a headache instead of curing one. They even made the sizes confusing. And, no free refills. It is without a doubt the most brilliant marketing strategy of the twentieth century: let's take something simple, cheap, and easy, and make it really complex and expensive. Done.

Here is another admission. Back in the *old days*—my youth—we never had wine with dinner. Ever. When I was young, I didn't even know people drank wine at dinner. And just so you don't think I was the only uncultured heathen in my town, no one else drank wine at dinner either. In fact, I didn't know of any family in my small-town-Tennessee neighborhood that drank wine at all, except for the family that had moved there from Italy. I heard they had wine with meals. *Strange*, I thought.

The only time I had ever had wine to drink, before I was thirty, was at communion in the Catholic church. We would sip of the "blood of Christ" after eating the "bread of life." Though I don't think this really counts as wine consumption.

That's not to say we didn't have drinkers. My dad had bourbon every night when he got home from work and beer on the weekends. People drank. They drank a lot. Just beer and hard liquor. Never wine.

Then suddenly, everyone drank wine. I mean *everyone*.

It was the thing you did when you went out to dinner, and then it became the thing you did at home. It became a national obsession it seemed: designer coffee in the morning and wine in the evening.

Suddenly, at every restaurant, I was handed a wine list with the menu. Wine racks started popping up on my friends' kitchen counters and over their refrigerators. Restaurants began touting their wine selections as much as their food. It was like we had all become European—overnight.

I find it all very puzzling because I still don't like the taste of wine. Whenever I voice this opinion, I always get the same answer: "It's an acquired taste. Once you start drinking it regularly, you will begin to like it." That's what they would all say.

Hmmm.

And why is it again that I would want to acquire a taste for something I never liked in the first place? I have never seen anyone trying to acquire a taste for dirt.

Why should I pay ten dollars a glass for something I

don't like when I can pay two dollars for a glass of iced tea that I would enjoy very much, plus not have to worry about getting a DUI on the way home? Call me crazy. I didn't get it.

I began to get pressured to drink wine when out for meals and I didn't like that at all. Then—as if that wasn't irritating enough—all these wine experts start popping up. Everywhere.

I'd see them sniff and twirl and swirl their wine around their glass and then their mouth as the waiter stood there at attention, holding the bottle at a forty-five-degree angle. This way the wine connoisseur could observe the label as they determined if the wine was bold enough, or oaky enough, or too dry or too sweet or too blah blah blah. I could vomit.

Yes, I am sure that some of the people doing this wine exercise might have some real expertise, but I would bet that a large percentage of them would not know oaky from sprucy.

How many times have you seen anyone send a wine back after the taste test? I never have. Well, except the time Sophia Petrillo sent her wine back on *The Golden Girls*, and that was only because she was trying to get out of paying for the bottle.

About the same time everyone was becoming a wine expert, they all suddenly also needed a gourmet kitchen at home. Electric ranges were now inferior and one had to have a gas range if you were any kind of cook at all. My mother churned out three meals a day of the best food you could want, for decades, on an electric range. But that no longer mattered. She didn't have a gas range, so she couldn't have been a good cook. No way.

I found it ironic that the people who desperately needed the gourmet kitchens almost never cooked at home. They were always out drinking coffee, or eating out at a restaurant with a fine glass of wine.

But nonetheless, when they did cook, it had to be on a gas range, and they needed the double oven and all the finest knives, pots, and gadgets—even if it was just to make pancakes.

When did it all get so complicated?

Maybe it happened the same time that pizza became flatbread, or when kale took the place of lettuce. I know trends come and go. And at least many of these trendy foods are healthier than the fast-food options of my youth. Still, it seems to me that we are very much in a pretentious-food-and-drink phase.

I just know that suddenly every salad had avocado in it, my fish was now blackened, and my tomatoes were now sun-dried. Cheese trays and cold cuts morphed into charcuterie boards. Then came bone marrow. Sounds disgusting to me, but I have seen it on more menus than I could count. Forgive my crassness, but I don't want to eat bone marrow. I don't care whose it is. Then pork belly seemed to be every restaurant's appetizer of choice. Oops, I meant *small plate* of choice.

This brings me to shared plates. Hate them.

Was it such a bad thing to just order a plate for yourself and not have to share it with everyone at the table? I never thought so. But now the first thing the server asks is, "What are we ordering for the table?" No longer can you just selfishly order what you want while the other diners do the same thing. Now we must order for the table.

And then begins the annoying countdown. The plate comes with seven croquettes and there are three people. What do you do? Everyone has two, and then there is that one left on the small shared plate. No one wants to take it, but everyone wants to eat it.

A discussion ensues.

"You eat it."

"No, you eat it, I insist."

"But I can't, I ate more of the pork belly."

"It's all yours! I couldn't eat another bite. I'll have some bone marrow in a minute."

And on and on and on.

Why do we have to suffer through this during what is supposed to be an enjoyable meal out? Can I not just order my own appetizer and entrée? Didn't that work for about a hundred years or so?

And why can't I sit at my own table with the people I chose to come to the restaurant with? Do we really need community tables? I know you must be thinking that I am an anti-social asshole. The real truth is that I like to be social when I *want* to be social. I want the *choice* to either sit with a group of strangers and be required to be social, or not. If this makes me an asshole, so be it, but I like my own food at my own table.

Of course, all this wine-swirling and tapas-counting is occurring at a restaurant that required me to valet park. When did parking your own car become such a big issue? If we were in New York, I would get it. In New York, I want valet parking. It is needed. But now every restaurant in Nashville seems to have it, and half the time your car is parked less than fifty feet away. Is it that difficult just to walk over to it? I could have easily parked it myself if I had been allowed to. But no, I had to valet. I know, pick your battles.

It seems this is another way in which we are trying to make ourselves something that we never knew we needed to be just a couple decades ago. I never felt that I grew up uncivilized or desperately in need of culture, but suddenly, everywhere I turn, our culture is changing, and we are being pressured into a more pretentious lifestyle.

For me, I'd rather skip all the wine and coffee and buy another piece of original art. That just makes so much more sense to me.

Growing up, I never knew anyone who collected original art—certainly not my parents or any of my friends' parents. But now I do. And I could easily buy a new painting for what many people spend on coffee and wine in just a few months. I could have a beautiful piece of original art that I would enjoy for a lifetime.

Wait a minute. Does this make me sound a little pretentious?

Well, damn.

I guess I'm just as bad as the wine and coffee snobs.

Maybe I should just order a board full of cheese and think about this.

OUTTA SPACE

Recently, a friend of mine was telling me about a cousin of hers who is a hoarder. It's been going on for years and is getting worse. The cousin is always talking about redecorating her house and making big plans, but can never execute anything because she would have to clear out some space first.

That doesn't stop her from trying, though.

She went to the furniture store, found a sofa she liked, and bought it on the spot. She told them to keep it in storage, just for a few weeks, until she could get her house cleaned out. She had no space to keep it right then, not even in her garage. They reluctantly agreed to hold it even though they thought it was strange since most people want the furniture delivered as soon as possible.

Months passed. Then years.

She told my friend that she was getting annoyed with the furniture company because they kept calling wanting her to take delivery of the sofa. This continued for two years until they demanded she take the sofa.

She decided the only thing to do was rent a mini-storage unit. My friend and I thought this meant that she would clean out her living room (storing her current furniture) to make space for the sofa. But no, we were mistaken. She had them deliver the new sofa to the mini-storage unit until she could clean out the living room. It is still sitting there.

We figure that by now she has spent about six thousand dollars—two thousand on the sofa and four thousand on storage—on a sofa she has yet to sit on.

I guess she is not the only one. These little storage-unit companies are popping up by the thousands—everywhere. Seems we love to keep our stuff.

I must admit, I love to get rid of stuff. It makes me feel good. That doesn't stop me from buying new stuff though. I like stuff like art and nice furniture. But when I find something I like better, I usually sell or donate the old version. I guess that puts me somewhere in the middle. Somewhere between the semi-hoarders of the world and the new generation of tiny-house dwellers.

I've been a designer for almost forty-years and I must tell you that this tiny-house trend is one I cannot understand or get behind. I watch these TV shows about tiny houses in a combination of shock and amazement.

They usually profile a family that has made the big, life-altering decision to downsize into a tiny home. Then the host and the carpenter build a new tiny home specifically for their needs.

These people are usually coming from a normal-sized home, typically around 1200 to 3000 square feet. They decide that the house it just too much of a burden—financial and otherwise—to keep. They say the rationale is that they want to have more *experiences* and less stuff in their lives. I get that.

So why don't they just downsize to a smaller house? Go from a 3000-square-foot house to a 1500-square-foot house, let's say. But no. According to the tiny-house people, that will never work. We must go from a full-size home to life in a closet—in one episode. They will adjust their big life to a little bitty tiny one, in a one-hour TV show.

I could understand a single person doing this. Or maybe even a married couple with no children doing this. But a family of four? Yes, they really do this. A family of four might move from a normal-sized ranch house into the equivalent of a walk-in closet.

I love how excited they act—at first—enthusiastically telling the viewers how this move is going to improve their lives dramatically. The togetherness. The love they will share—all of them in that one room.

Everyone is up for the adventure until they inform the kids that they will have to pick only one or two toys from their collection of a hundred. Then the kids' faces turn from big smiles to skeptical grimaces. The cameras cut away quickly.

The designers then force them to get rid of all non-essential items—which is basically everything they own.

As they build the home, they point out a lot of multi-use items and spaces. And there is nothing wrong with that, except that you generally always have to move something in order to do something else. For instance, you have to lift up the bed in order to expose your home office—which incidentally is usually a plank of wood barely large enough to place a laptop. The owners act surprised and delighted until they realize there is nowhere to put their printer.

Also, I wonder what will happen when one spouse has the flu and wants to stay in bed all day while the other spouse works from home. I suppose he can crawl up under the bed and use his laptop.

In each tiny home there is usually a somewhat normal kitchen: it has a sink, maybe a small range, and a small refrigerator. They might have a few feet of counter space, but never much. The few cabinets are filled to the max with the basic cooking needs. This is necessary because most of the tiny-home dwellers opt to live out in the middle of nowhere so they can experience nature. Some even homeschool their children.

There are no bedrooms. Sleeping occurs on a mattress in a tiny loft space, at the top of a ladder. The producers of the show, incidentally, never film anyone putting the linens on this bed. This will require a contortionist—a fact that will be discovered soon enough by the new dwellers. But never, ever, shown in the episode.

The children's bedrooms involve pulling down a bunk from a wall or folding down the dining table to make a bed.

There is only one tiny bathroom containing a toilet, usually with the shower above it, and a sink—no vanity—for everyone to share. You cannot be modest living in one of these tiny homes. The bathroom is just a few feet from the kitchen and the sleeping and living areas.

By far, my favorite thing about the tiny-home episodes, is when they talk about storage. These people have usually moved out of a house with five or six good-sized closets, and now they are basically in a camper with no closets whatsoever. The designers excitedly show the new owners all of the "massive" three linear feet of hanging space that the entire family can now share for their clothes. Since they have been forced to give away the bulk of their wardrobe during the episode, their clothes will fit in the space—for now.

The hosts then show the family the "huge" storage bins under the sofa that will house their shoes and maybe some of the children's toys. The designer goes on and on about the storage space behind the bathroom sink (that might hold three towels and a couple of bottles of shampoo) and the pantry that is the size of a medium-sized Igloo ice chest.

I can't recall ever seeing any laundry facilities in these tiny homes, but you really shouldn't need them anyway. You have virtually no clothes left after the big downsizing, and you can just beat those on a rock at the always-nearby stream.

The owners seem to buy into all this downsizing as if their lives will suddenly become non-materialistic, and they will never buy another thing. Actually, they can't buy anything. There is not a spot anywhere to put it. In every episode I have seen, all the storage spaces are totally maxed out the day they move in. But you and I know they will buy more things.

Children grow and they get bigger and they need bigger toys. They also need baseball uniforms and hockey equipment, and since they are living by the lake, someone is going to want water toys. Then, of course, you need swim suits and picnic supplies and each child will need a computer for schoolwork, and you will need space for arts and crafts projects.

Heaven forbid, someone decides to take up a hobby. If they do, the hobby will need to be painting scenes on the top of a pinhead, or something like that. There certainly is no room to store canvases or an easel.

I always want them to revisit these families and see what they do when they realize that the quality life they wanted so desperately to have in these tiny homes can only take place if they all become monks. There simply isn't room in their home to store anything, or for anything new.

But it isn't just the problem of buying new things.

Let's say they never buy new things. There still isn't room to exercise, or practice a new dance move or entertain friends—at least not that I can see. What if the daughter wants to go to a prom? There isn't a closet that would accommodate a full-length gown.

I suppose you do learn to get along as a family— really, there is no choice. There is nowhere to run if you have an argument. You have to stay in the same room and work it out because there is not another room in which to go sulk.

I wonder if they remain in the tiny homes for life? I wonder if it is what they thought it would be?

I know I could get by in so much less space, and I could survive as a single person in a tiny home if I needed to. But in the case of a married couple, does this make a marriage stronger—or bring out the flaws?

Really, I guess I should be paying more attention to these TV shows because it occurs to me that as I age —and my clients age—rather than getting calls to design new larger homes, I might begin getting calls from clients wanting help with downsizing. Maybe they will be moving to smaller, one-level homes or retirement village apartments. I would be happy to do that. I love any kind of design project. And making small spaces feel larger is one of my favorite design challenges.

It also occurs to me that I will probably be designing a tiny home for myself in the future. Maybe at a retirement home or in an assisted-living community. I hope I am not resistant to giving up my stuff when the time comes. I think I can deal with the material loses, like art and furniture and such, but when I hit the age when I need to downsize, there is just one thing I surely don't want to lose: my mind.

That's something I want to hang on to.

TABLE FOR ONE

It's Saturday morning and I am sitting in a booth at the little breakfast place that's just a few blocks from my Nashville condo. Going out to breakfast on the weekend is one of my favorite things to do. Most of the time I go alone. I just get up, throw on some clothes, and head over for an omelet and some good wheat toast with blackberry jam.

Nothing fancy.

The restaurant is part of a chain that I first discovered in Savannah, Georgia. I had been telling them for years (when I visited Savannah and ate there) that they should open one in Nashville. Finally, about ten years later, they did, and it was within walking distance from my condo. I was so excited I almost wrecked my car when I saw the sign.

This particular morning, I was working my crossword puzzle on my phone (I try to get it done between the time I place my order and they time they bring my food, but usually don't) and I couldn't help but overhear this fairly loud conversation coming from the next booth. It caught my attention because it was exactly the conversation you always hear about from the sister of the missing woman on *Forensic Files*.

I might be a little bit obsessed with true crime shows.

You know the scenario. An older widow is lonely. An attractive gentleman—usually claiming he's former military, an ex-Admiral, or such—comes into her life from another city and sweeps her off her feet. His background seems quite mysterious to all of her friends and family, but she assures them that he is the real deal and that they are deeply in love.

Then she disappears. The disappearance doesn't occur, however, until she has married him and changed the beneficiary on all her life insurance policies.

Sometimes they find the body and sometimes they don't, but either way, she is never heard from again.

This man in the next booth—the "future killer" I will call him—is laughing, and flattering her (the "future victim"), and then laughing more. It all sounds so fake, so forced. It sounds like a first date, one where he is trying really, really hard. She is engaged in the conversation, but it is really all about him. He is doing all the bragging, talking about the trips he wants to take her on and all the places they will see—*together*. I think if I followed them around the rest of the day, I would surely see some type of ultra-romantic marriage proposal. Maybe at Centennial Park, in front of the Parthenon, on one knee, using a ring he has purchased with money he's already scammed from her bank account.

At this same breakfast, another couple was seated at the booth right beside me. In the midst of all this talking from the other booth, it took a few moments for me to notice them, but they caught my attention because they were equally interesting. Within a minute-and-a-half, I had already determined with great assurance that she had been a mail-order bride. She was a young, foreign beauty with long dark hair and dark eyes. She was wearing large, tinted glasses. Maybe in her early thirties. He was a good thirty years older, with disheveled gray hair and kind of a grumpy, unkempt look. I think the purchase had probably occurred a decade or so ago because they seemed quite at ease—and pretty bored—with one another.

She ordered in very broken English, then he ordered, and then they proceeded to not speak another word. Finally, when the food came, I think it gave them a reason to speak a few words, but this didn't seem like the kind of relationship that was built on mutual interests or deep conversation. It definitely seemed transactional in nature. Not that there is anything wrong with that. They may both be very happy and content. I just couldn't help but notice.

That's one of the reasons I like dining and traveling alone. The things you notice. I made sure to take some very good mental pictures of the other couple, because when *Forensic Files* does the episode about them, I feel sure they will need me to be the "casual-observer witness" that is always interviewed somewhere in between the grieving sister and the family members of the killer's other victims. I could speak about the day I saw him working his charms on her and how, from the start, I knew he was up to no good.

Breakfast is not always this interesting.

As a matter of fact, most days, I don't even notice the people around me. I am usually reading the news on my phone, or doing crosswords in an attempt to stave off Alzheimer's disease.

I also really enjoy talking to the servers. They are usually college students from Belmont University, which is right around the corner. I like hearing about their studies and the plans they have for the future. I also like the fact that many of them seem to see me more as a peer than as an old man. We exchange notes on the projects we are working on and they even ask my advice on things. Maybe they are just looking for tips, but I don't think that's the case, at least not always.

I've gotten to know some of them pretty well, and I really look forward to seeing them when I stop in.

Nick is studying sound engineering, but that got derailed during COVID. We've tossed around the idea of recording some stories from my book, but haven't yet. He is a very small-framed, young guy with tousled blonde hair. His cobra tattoo circles around and around his arm, with a mouth opened-to-strike positioned right over the thumb and first finger joint. There are a pair of dice involved in the tattoo as well, coming out of the cobra's mouth, I believe.

I'm worried about Nick, though. He smokes for one thing. But the thing that really worries me is that he keeps talking about this bad chest congestion he can't get rid of. I asked him how long it had been bothering him and he said, "About a year-and-a-half."

"Good Lord, Nick," I said, "have you been to the doctor?" Of course, he had not. Young people never take care of themselves. They believe they will live forever and most of them don't have a doctor anyway. I told him to go to a walk-in clinic and at least get a chest x-ray. He said he would. I hope he does. I guess I'll find out next weekend.

It was definitely a busy morning at the breakfast place. Before I left, a couple came in that I always enjoy seeing. They must both be in their early eighties. The wife is in an electric wheelchair with what appears to be only minimal use of her hands and legs. She is always nicely dressed and well-groomed with a short gray bob. Her husband is a tall, slim, ginger-headed man—always smiling—who follows her to their regular table. The staff removes a chair from the table as they enter the restaurant, and the couple easily takes their place for breakfast.

Unlike the mail-order couple, the octogenarians carry on a casual conversation all through their meal and chat a lot with the servers. I think about how much assistance the husband must give his wife to get ready for this little outing, helping her with bathing, dressing, and getting in and out of the car. He always seems to be happy, and I have no doubt he is equally cheerful during the time they are getting ready. It always makes me smile to watch them, knowing they have probably been together over fifty years—almost as long as I have been alive—and knowing that they face any obstacle together.

It would really be nice to have someone like that, with that long history and comfort level, to share meals and to travel with, but I've never found that person. So I learned many, many years ago that if I wanted to do things, I would need to do a lot of them alone. When I was very young, I would be self-conscious about eating out by myself, or going to a show alone. I thought people were staring at me, thinking I had no friends and was a weirdo.

Well, the truth of the matter is that I *am* kind of weird, and some people do stare at you just because you are out eating alone.

It's not that I don't have friends. I have lots of friends.

But I am also the kind of person that would rather go somewhere alone than ask a good friend to go to an event that I know they don't want to attend. To ask a friend to suffer because I don't want to go alone just seems a bit inconsiderate.

I am also a bit selfish when I am traveling. I like to set my own agenda, pick my own restaurants, and stroll at my own pace. Traveling with a group can really be challenging. It seems you barely finish one meal before the same tired old conversation starts again.

Person A: "What are we doing for dinner?"

Person B: "I don't really care."

Person C: "Well, I saw a cute, little Italian restaurant that I would like to try."

Person D: "Oh, really? I was kind of thinking about that sushi place we walked by today."

Person B: "I don't like sushi."

Person A: "Italian sounds good to me."

Person B: "Italian seems heavy, can't we do something lighter?"

Person A: "Well, Person B, why don't you suggest somewhere."

Person B: "Oh no, you guys choose. I really don't care where we go."

And on and on and on.

The worst thing that can happen is to realize that you

are on a trip with Person B. They can never be pleased. They will never make a decision. But they will freely criticize every decision that is made by the group. Person B can make any trip feel like an eternity.

It is also inevitable that anytime you have a group of four or more, you will have at least one Person B. You might leave home with six travelers, but after a few days, you are hoping to return with only five.

I do often travel with friends (hopefully exclusive of the Person-B types) and I enjoy that very much. Just as often, though, I travel alone, and I enjoy that just the same. Or, I must confess, sometimes I enjoy it more.

I think our society programs us to think that there is something wrong with traveling alone. At first, I felt self-conscious about it. But I also didn't want to miss out on these experiences. So I changed my attitude, and I hit the road. I have found that being out-and-about alone simply means you are confident in your own skin, not that you are lonely.

The first trip I took alone was to London. I was twenty-eight. I had been to Europe before, and I always wanted to visit England. My parents had just been to London and talked about how clean and beautiful it was, so I felt this would be a great trip for me. The first production of *The Phantom of the Opera* had been playing there for a few years, but had not yet toured, so I had never seen it. And I really wanted to see it.

Everything about London appealed to me. The beautifully maintained buildings, the sense of tradition, the noticeable cleanliness of it all. And the taxis all matched. All of the taxis were these cool, retro-style, black sedans, and the taxi drivers were traveling encyclopedias of the city streets. And they were so friendly.

I would take bus tours out into the stunning countryside during the day to visit places like Canterbury, Oxford, Windsor, and Salisbury. On those rides, the countryside looked like a patchwork quilt, with each crop a different color, bordered by a hedge fence. The simple little stone homes with thatched roofs appeared to be straight out of a Disney movie.

After those daytime trips, I would be back in the city in time to grab a bite to eat and go see a show in the evening. I had no idea London had so much theater to choose from, but it was comparable to New York. (I didn't know this because I had not been to New York yet, but I discovered this later.) I saw four shows on that trip, and they all were great. After I saw *Phantom*, I didn't want to get on the tube (the subway) to go back to my hotel. I needed to walk and process what I had seen.

The city is lit beautifully at night and I distinctly remember humming the tunes from the show as I wandered the empty streets home. It was a long walk, but I felt no fatigue—a combination of being twenty-eight years old and feeling a sense of euphoria. It was probably about midnight when I got to the hotel. It occurred to me, then, that I would probably be traveling solo a lot in the future.

And I did.

The last big trip I took alone was right before the COVID shutdown. I had signed-up for a Broadway cruise. I had heard about them and it sounded right up my alley: a traditional cruise ship where Broadway aficionados are a small sub-group of the passengers. Obviously, there aren't enough Broadway nerds like myself to fill the three thousand slots the ship would hold. I think there were about a hundred and fifty of us.

You are on board with the host, Seth Rudetsky, and several Tony Award-winning performers. At night each star does a solo show, and during the day there are trivia contests, master classes, and rehearsals. It was a really strange feeling for me. I've never been on a trip with so many people that had the same passion I had. It was kind of a utopia for me. I couldn't have cared less about the islands we stopped at. I just was loving all the activities and the talk about favorite musicals and songs and actors.

I was a bit concerned at the beginning of the trivia contests because I was in a group of equally enthusiastic musical theater nuts. I did, however, kick butt. They even quit calling on me after a while because they thought they should let some others have a shot. I thought that was a crock of shit. I had a lifetime of (usually useless) Broadway knowledge I had been waiting to access and, as far as I was concerned, these other people needed to step-up or step-overboard. There was another guy that beat me in a couple of rounds, but he was in the front row and got called on more than I did, so I am going to be generous to him and call it a tie.

What did intimidate me, though, were the rehearsals. During the week, the cruisers would learn the back-up parts for a song with each of the Broadway stars. On the final night there, there would be a variety show, and the passengers would perform with the star. I am not a trained singer. Not at all. I can carry a tune, but that's about it. Most of the others were experienced and trained. Man, could they sing. It was amazing. This was a room full of music teachers, community-theater actors, directors, and frustrated singers. So, they were ready to let go. When we first sang as a group, I was blown away. We sounded fantastic.

Even though I had a great deal of difficulty staying on my part, this was fun for me. Everyone was so helpful and so kind. I was really enjoying the singing, until the fifth day…when he sprung *choreography* on us.

Yes, there would be steps to accompany the background vocals. I barely had my music down and now I had to move? At the same time? This took way too much mental focus. I just could not get it down. No way. I determined quickly that I could either sing or move, but not both at the same time.

Some of the young girls in the group had the steps down on the first run-through. You could tell they had dance backgrounds. I wanted to slap them.

I have always had so much respect for the performers on the Broadway stage, but this made me see them in an entirely new light. I was exhausted after every rehearsal, and we only rehearsed an hour. Real performers would work that hard all day. I decided then and there that I would stick to writing.

That trip was so eye-opening in so many ways. On the first day, I met a group of people and we became fast friends. We did almost everything together for the rest of the trip. I still keep in touch with most of them.

I'm smiling now as I think about that trip. I had a ball.

I also smile when I think about that first trip to London. I went back to London for my thirtieth birthday, and I've been back to London many times since then. I've had fun every time I returned, but none like that first time. That first London trip set me on a life-long course of independence and discovery. It has been way too many years since I have been there, though. I am itching to go back once more.

Until I make that next trip, if you see me out eating alone, don't think I'm lonely. I'm enjoying my own company. I'm probably thinking about another story, or another place I want to visit. You might even be doing, or saying, something that gives me an idea.

On the other hand, if you are a *Forensic Files* "future victim" or "future killer" (like the man at the next table), it certainly will make my breakfast much more interesting. I'll probably make a mental note about you for a new story.

But of course, I'd rather you not be. I really don't want to testify at your trial. It's a lot of pressure, and I might be traveling.

AT WIT'S END

I was just putting the final touches on my second book (this one) when I got a text from Jay's mother. This text was one that I had been dreading for a long time. Jay was in the final stages of a years-long battle with cancer, and it was very near the end. His mother was letting me know he had been moved to palliative care.

I said all the cuss words I could think of.

It didn't help.

I knew it was coming, but somehow I could not allow myself to believe that Jay, someone so filled with life, could no longer be alive. And yet here I was, only a week or so later, at his funeral. The church was packed. Full of family, friends, and loved ones.

My whole family liked Jay a lot. We got to know him when his mom came to work at our family construction business. He would stop by to see her, and we would end up in conversation about something.

You really couldn't help but like Jay. He would do odd jobs and yard work for me and for my parents to make college money. He was witty, smart, unfiltered, and had a tremendous work ethic. He and I clicked immediately, and that was very unusual for me. In Boonetown, I didn't easily *click* with people.

But Jay was completely himself and comfortable in his own skin. He didn't mind bragging about an accomplishment, and his sarcastic comments were sort of a trademark. In our talks, I discovered that Jay was very much into design and art and architecture, so we had a lot in common. He thought I had the best taste—and who was I to disagree?

He would wash my mom's car every week or so in the summer. He told me that he really liked working for my mom because she was so down-to-earth and treated him as an equal, not as a hired hand. Jay also told me, on many occasions over the years, that he knew he was going to like my mom the day she referred to this woman in town as a "sanctimonious bitch." Nobody really liked this woman because, well, Mom was accurate in her assessment, and this endeared my mom to Jay immediately. He liked that my mom called a spade a spade. Jay also called a spade a spade. Sanctimonious-bitch became sort of a go-to term for Jay and me in the years that followed.

Before Jay married, he would house-sit for me when I would go on trips. He was still living at home with his parents at the time, so it gave him some privacy. I didn't really need a house-sitter, but I had just built a new house and he really liked it—a lot. I loved it when he would house-sit because he would leave my place cleaner than he found it and in perfect order.

When I came back from the first trip, he told me that he would sweep my front terrace and have his coffee out there every morning. I told him that really wasn't necessary—that much sweeping—and he said, "Oh no, I just do it so that people driving by will think it's my house." I was flattered—and also the beneficiary of a very clean front terrace.

When I first knew Jay, he was at Vanderbilt, getting an engineering degree. He was about eight years younger than I was. After Jay graduated, he focused on two things: one, having a successful career, and two, getting married and having a family. There was no question in his mind where he was going and what he would do. He was determined. And, of course, he achieved his goals.

Jay actually married my first cousin. He told me when they first started dating, and he seemed to be quite serious about her. Before long they were married and began a beautiful family, eventually having three children. I saw Jay less and less during those years. He was very busy being a good husband and father. When we did see each other, though, it was always as if no time had passed. We would always have big laughs before the conversation ended. We both saw things from a similarly warped vantage point.

After that text from his mom, I couldn't get him off my mind, so I went for a walk on Scarritt Bennett Campus. The campus abuts the parking lot of my Nashville condo. Scarritt Bennett was once a Methodist College that is now a retreat center. It's pretty much empty most of the time. I love it there. I am able to walk there freely. It is without doubt (at least to me) the prettiest college campus in Nashville.

It occurred to me how much Jay would love it here. It is the only campus I have ever been on where all the buildings are the of same architectural style and built with the same materials. The buildings have various combinations of design elements, but they blend beautifully. All of them are gothic masterpieces, with slate roofs and copper gutters that have been green for decades. The stone buildings are beautifully connected by arched-ceiling porticos and stone walkways. As I walked, I wondered if Jay had ever walked this campus while he was at Vandy—surely he did. It's right next door. I can't believe we never discussed it.

During his years of tests and diagnoses and hospital stays, we began to speak a lot more often. He was spending a lot of time taking treatments and waiting for doctor's appointments, so he had more time to chat. I was constantly amazed by him. He never complained about the tests, or the pain, or all the time away from his family. I can only imagine how much I would complain. Or at least I'd want to discuss it a lot. He never did. He would just send me something silly and make me laugh. As his body was being attacked on many fronts, his sense of humor remained in-tact. He never felt sorry for himself, and he never lost hope.

He would often send me crazy photos he found online. It was usually when someone got really "creative" and took a fairly nice piece of furniture and up-cycled it into something truly hideous. He'd send photos of some reproduction Mediterranean end tables that had been painted purple, and say he was having them delivered to my home for my birthday. Or maybe he would just send a photo of a tag on a pair of Levi's that read, "Size 62 x 32 Athletic Fit" with the caption, "Athletic, really?" One picture he sent was of a stack of old used tires that had been converted into a wishing well. "You just can't buy this kind of originality," he would say. We had a great time being design snobs.

During all of the sickness, all of the ups and downs, he was still focused on being the best father, husband, and citizen possible. He was still attending his children's school events, cooking for friends or working at his church. He never wasted time and he never quit laughing.

It isn't fair—dying at age fifty-three—but the sad reality is that he is gone. I cannot imagine how immense this loss is for his family and for those closest to him. I certainly feel a great sense of loss, as do all those that knew him. He left a big empty space in this world that, honestly, I'm not sure can be filled.

I sure hope I run into Jay again—in the next life. I know we will pick up right where we left off. I can just imagine the first thing he will say. Something like, "Were you at my funeral? It was standing room only."

PARIS AT NIGHT

It was late in the day when we arrived—in Paris. My first time in Paris. My first time in Europe. My first time out of the United States. This was definitely a trip full of firsts.

I was pretty overwhelmed by the whole thing. We had no reservations, and I had absolutely no idea where I was or what I was doing. I could not speak French and, therefore, could not read the signs. I was getting more and more nervous.

I was with my oldest friend. We had met in the first grade and had been best friends for years. He had decided to become a priest and graduated from a seminary in Iowa at the same time I graduated from the University of North Alabama. He decided to attend major seminary in Belgium. I barely knew where Belgium was, and I didn't even know what language they spoke there. (As I recall, it was an American seminary, so they spoke English in their classes.) But the whole thing seemed very intimidating to me. He was always more adventurous than I was, though, and he was excited by the prospect of showing me Paris.

This was in 1984. There was no internet then. We only communicated via the mail: old-fashioned letter writing. Jeff had already traveled a lot in Europe during his first year there. Groups of seminarians would head out on breaks to cities like Paris and London, or maybe head over into Germany for some sight-seeing. I could not believe the places Jeff had already seen in his time there. So, when he invited me to come over for a couple of weeks and tour with him, I was both excited and a little nervous to go.

Jeff was my personal tour guide. And even though he didn't speak the languages—and we didn't have any itinerary or plans—he did a great job and packed more adventures into two weeks than I could have imagined. The first few days, I stayed in the seminary in Belgium with Jeff and the other seminarians that were in residence. We spent those days roaming around Louvain and then Brussels.

Brussels was really beautiful, but I loved all the European cities we visited. The architecture was stunning. Everything was so old and yet so well-preserved. Back home we couldn't even save our one-hundred-year-old courthouse from the wrecking ball. Our city fathers never invested in maintenance on any buildings, not even the courthouse, so it sadly hit the ground the year I graduated from the eighth grade. In Europe, it was not unusual to be in a four- or five-hundred-year-old building. I loved the warmth and the character in these well-worn structures, structures that are still standing because they are appreciated and cared-for.

We arrived in Paris in the early evening, as I recall, and discovered we were in the midst of fashion-show season. There wasn't a room to be found anywhere. We were on foot, carrying our luggage, and there were no cell phones or internet sites to search for rooms. We just had to pound the cobblestones and ask at each place in person. I realized quickly that I had packed too much. I had not gotten the memo back then that you were supposed to backpack through Europe.

Earlier, we had met two girls on the train who were around twenty-years-old. They had taken a year off to travel after graduating high school. I had never heard of this. According to them, everyone from their country did this, as did many Europeans. I want to think they were from Norway, but don't hold me to that. I just know that they were backpacking across Europe with just the essentials and eating a lot of bread and tomato sandwiches to get by cheaply. They could speak English fluently, which always makes me feel uneducated when I travel abroad.

Had I met them sooner I might have made better packing choices, but I was very green as far as travel goes. Up until that time, the biggest trip I had ever been on was when my parents took us to Florida for ten excruciating days. I think I was in the sixth grade then.

Florida was hot. Very hot. The travel-trailer that my parents and sister stayed in was air-conditioned. The whole family used to stay in that small trailer, but that was just for a quick trip to a nearby state park for maybe three days. This was a ten-day trip to Florida, and Dad thought the trailer was too crowded for the five of us. So, he bought one of those camper tops to go on the bed of his new pickup truck. This was not an actual camper like you see on some pickup trucks. This was merely a thin, un-insulated, metal lid over the bed of the truck, something most people used just to keep their tools and equipment dry.

He installed two small, wood-framed cots, one on each side of the truck bed. Our new traveling prison cell was complete. Complete with *no* air-conditioning. My brother and I couldn't get along in an air-conditioned bedroom four times this size, so you just knew this tin can was a good idea. Not only did we have to sleep there, we had to ride all the way there and all the way back on those cots. I feel sure that, by today's standards, this would be considered child abuse. But this was a different time.

We spent many, many hours on those cots—sweating. We finally did make it to the new Disney World theme park that had only been open a couple of years. The whole family was really excited about it but, sadly, the main thing I remember was long, long lines. Hours and hours standing in long lines. There were no passes or reservations either. These were the early, primitive days of Disney. Some of the rides turned out to be a lot of fun, but after waiting an hour or two to get on them no one was anxious to take another spin.

We also made it to Cypress Gardens and Cape Canaveral (both of which were really cool as I recall), and I am sure a few other places but those escape my memory. Most of all, though, I remember the long, hot ride there and back—and, of course, sweating.

That was the last trip I recall us taking as a family. I think my parents were permanently scarred. The camper was retired to the back yard for good.

So I am not being dramatic when I say I had no travel experience during any of my teen years. When I first arrived in Paris, everything was new to me.

After several hours of searching—first carrying and then dragging our luggage—finally, down a little side street, we found a room in a charming little hotel on the third or fourth floor. I bet there weren't more than twenty rooms in the entire place. There were no elevators, but at least we had a private bath.

I say *charming*, but I really don't remember much about it. It was very old, but we had a cute little Juliette balcony and twin beds. It could have been filthy and I would have been happy. Just to have a place to put my luggage was foremost on my mind.

By then, it was late in the evening. I was exhausted and figured we might make an early night of it, but Jeff was excited to show me the city. So we dropped our bags in the room and took off.

I can't recall much about the area we were staying in, and I'm not sure how far we were from Notre Dame Cathedral, but we made our way there on foot and took in the spectacular view of this masterpiece at night.

Then, as I recall, we made our way through the Tuileries Gardens and then on to the Champs-Élysées. We strolled up the famous avenue, stopping at one of the cafes along the way for hot chocolate.

I knew that Paris was known as the City of Light, but I was not prepared for what I was seeing. It seemed like everything was glowing. It was a beautiful night too. The sky was clear and it was fairly warm. Trees were lit with stands of lights, and the street lamps cast a shadowy glow. It was just as you wanted it to be — magical.

Since that night, I have been to many places with grand build-ups and great accolades of their beauty. A lot of them did not live up to the hype. Paris did — and beyond. The combination of my lack of travel experience, my first time being in a major European city, and seeing these sights at night created an almost dream-like state. A sensory overload.

We continued up the Champs-Élysées, and we could see the magnificent Arc de Triomphe aglow in the distance. As we made our way toward it, the glow became warmer and brighter, drawing us in. All I could think was that whoever was in charge of lighting up Paris definitely knew what they were doing. Of course, it helps to have glorious monuments, beautiful parks and breathtaking architecture to work with. Paris had that in abundance.

Taking our lives into our hands, we skirted through the busy traffic and stood under the towering arch. We eventually made our way to the Eiffel Tower. It was gloriously lit as well. Jeff insisted we go to the top and take in the view. It was about midnight by the time we stood atop that beautiful structure. The entire city was glowing and twinkling and welcoming us to Paris. It is one of my favorite memories of any trip.

We spent the next few days in Paris taking in even more sights: The Palace and the grounds at Versailles, The Sacré Coeur Basilica, Notre Dame, The Louvre Museum and more. Each and every one stunning. For an architecture geek like myself, Paris stands at the top of the list of must-see places. I hear that Prague is comparable, but I haven't managed to get there to compare.

I hated to leave Paris. There was so much more to see and do, but there was also much more ahead on that trip. The French Rivera and Monte Carlo were both beautiful. In Italy, we spent time in Florence and finally Rome. All of these cities had their own charm, amazing museums, and fabulous architecture.

I have been back to Paris since that trip, always wanting to experience the thrill of that first night again. But it wasn't ever the same. For sure, the sights were still breathtaking and beautiful, but on those return trips I had unreasonable expectations. I knew it would be impossible to recreate that first time I saw Paris, on foot, at night.

So I will just hold on to that memory of when it was all new to me and so very exciting, my memory of a city filled with all the beauty and architectural wonder I could ever hope for. All aglow in warm light, seemingly just for me.

QUALITY TIME

The head cook immediately came over and told me—in a not-so-quiet way—that the grilled-cheese sandwich *was* on Nell's plate when she put it down. The cook said, "*Someone* talked her out of it."

I could see that right now the grilled-cheese was on LaDonna's plate. And LaDonna was the only other person at the table, so it wasn't really difficult to figure out who had talked Nell out of it.

The cook and I sort of glared at LaDonna. LaDonna said to the cook and me, in her most innocent voice, "You are making me look like the villain." We both looked at her with an *are-you-kidding?* face.

About that time another lady (who sits with a different resident at The Peak Assisted Living community) came over to the table. "I need to talk to you," she said. I stood up and moved away from the table.

She said, "I saw the whole thing. LaDonna sat right there and talked your Aunt Nell out of her grilled-cheese."

Apparently, the moment the cook set the sandwich down, the cook told LaDonna that it was made for Nell. LaDonna then lied and said she had ordered one. But the cook said, no, that her nephew (me) had ordered it for Nell and if LaDonna wanted one, she needed to tell the kitchen by three p.m.

I said, "Well, I figured as much."

The lady was clearly angry.

She went on to say, "LaDonna used to sit at our table and we can't stand her. She is a manipulative liar. I just wanted you to know that I saw the whole thing—in case you need a witness."

I didn't plan to press charges or anything. So, I didn't really need a witness, but it was good to have my suspicion confirmed.

When I sat back down at the table, LaDonna sat right there and ate every bite of my sweet Aunt Nell's grilled-cheese sandwich. Right there, in front of me and Nell and God. What a bitch.

Aunt Nell had been very sick with pneumonia and this was her first trip to the dining room since she had been diagnosed. We had always tried to steer Nell away from LaDonna, but Nell, at age eighty-seven, was suffering with dementia, and she just loved LaDonna. So by this time we had given up the fight.

LaDonna was conniving to say the least. And when she got caught in a lie—which she often did—she would try to come off as an innocent angel.

My buddies at The Peak made no bones about their dislike of LaDonna. That's saying a lot. At The Peak, I was always amazed by the kind and caring staff. My aunt received exceptional care and the staff loved her. This made them dislike LaDonna even more when she pulled one of her tricks. This grilled-cheese-sandwich maneuver, on the heels of Nell's serious illness, put them all in fighting mode. They were mad. The next day they were still talking about it.

When my aunt first told me about LaDonna, she was in awe. She would tell me about the radio talk show LaDonna used to host and the plane she had piloted. Nell mentioned LaDonna's world travels and her PhD's (she had more than one). LaDonna, according to herself, had done it all and would brag about it constantly to Nell. Nell was too kind to ever question it. She has always been a person who believed the best about everyone. So LaDonna had found the perfect chum for her time in assisted living.

I was skeptical of LaDonna from the start because she would rush to tell me those same stories. I knew at least some of it had to be made up. Later some of my informants verified that it was all a big load of crap. No talk shows. No piloting a plane. No PhD's.

Several years prior to this, Aunt Nell was still living at her home. My sister, Janice, and I had begun to notice her increasing forgetfulness and weight loss. We also discovered that she was not taking her medicine properly.

Then we noticed that she would spend the afternoon roaming around stores like Kroger and Walgreens. She had never been much of a shopper. We began to wonder what could be causing this behavior. We suspected it was because she was lonely at home. She had never married and had no children.

I hadn't been inside her house in a while. She would always say, "Oh, my place is a mess, I'll just meet you there." Janice sort of forced her way into Nell's house one day and discovered things had really taken a turn. She had started hoarding. Well, I'm not sure it was *hoarding*, but definitely a lot of repetitive buying. Whatever it was, it was bad.

My sister began going over to her house with the pretense of helping her "straighten-up", but it turned out to be a much larger operation than that. Nell was very resistant to getting rid of things, so it had to be done gradually.

For example, over the course of many clean-up days, Janice found 32 cans of Pledge and 22 bottles of Fantastic. It became obvious the shopping trips were just an excuse to socialize. And in order to not look out of place, we guessed she would buy things, forgetting she already had an ample supply at home. She would just lay the bag of items down when she got home and over time, things had really piled up.

She had also gotten lost several times while out driving which worried us a lot. She was still coming to meet me every day for lunch, so I knew she was ok, but her usually pristine personal appearance was beginning to change. Her confusion would be better some days and worse others.

We knew it was time to do something. Assisted living seemed like the best solution. We also knew it would be a hard sell, but now this was a safety and health issue. It had to be done.

She loved her little house.

For years she had talked about this very cute little house on one of the streets where she walked for her daily exercise. Then, one day as she walked by, she saw that it was on the market. It was owned by another single lady who had never married, and I think Nell felt it was meant for her. I knew she would always regret it if she didn't buy it so I pushed her pretty hard to make the purchase. She was so happy when it was finally hers. It wasn't that she was into home décor or design like I was. She really didn't care about that at all. She just wanted a home to call her very own after years and years of renting.

Twenty years or so had passed since she bought that house, and now we were faced with a big decision. We had heard great things about The Peak, and a studio apartment unit was available. Just one room with a bath and closet, but it had large windows and the price was all inclusive.

We carefully chose what furnishings would fit best and mean the most to her. My sister spent days helping her go through things and get ready to move. We had decided to go with the premise that the move would only be for the winter months, hoping this would ease her into the transition and praying that she would be happy there. We both thought she would love all the activities and socialization.

We prepped the room in advance so it was all ready for her move, but on the day of the move it was still traumatic for my sister and me, and for Nell. Looking back I think Janice and I were even *more* traumatized than Nell.

Ever since her move, I have joked with my friends about what I might take to The Peak if I have to move there someday. Right off, I knew that I would have to have a two-room suite. The one-room scenario would just drive me nuts. I'd have to have a place to have a table or desk to eat at and to draw on. Then I'd need some bookshelves for all my design books and theater biographies. The metal slimline bookcases from Room and Board would be best because they are open and airy and fit most anywhere. I'd also want at least one of my antique English chests for storage and to add some warmth.

The real problem would be art. I collect art, and I have some really good paintings. A lot of them, actually. Pairing down my collection would be tough. Really tough.

And of course, I'd want my California-king adjustable bed. The only bed I've ever had that my feet didn't hang off of. I realize this would be a problem. It would literally be wall-to-wall in the compact bedrooms there. But I really think in assisted living I should have a bed that contains both me and my feet.

It has become a joke with me and my friend Maggie. I'll be in my house, maybe moving some furniture around, and I'll say, "This will definitely go to The Peak" or "This won't make the cut." It's become our little shorthand for how much we like something.

Fortunately for Nell, and for us, it was a very quick adjustment. She loved it.

After only a few days she was in the middle of every activity and never to be found in her room. I was elated and so relieved.

I would go to visit her and she would be fidgeting the whole time. I'd ask what was wrong and she would say, "Target practice is at 2 o'clock," and I'd say, "Well, it's only 1:30," to which she would respond, "Yes, but if you get there late you have to sit farther away from the target and it's harder to score high." I got so tickled. To hear her talking about target practice and bingo and cards and games and all the things they were doing was such an unexpected joy. She was having fun, loving the staff and many—if not all — of the other residents.

Her mental state improved. She began to gain weight and looked so much healthier. It was just what she needed and it was such a relief to us to know that she was well taken care of.

She had always worried about everyone else and never thought about herself. I will admit that her extreme selflessness was sometimes a great source of frustration to me.

She really had very low self-esteem, and it made me so sad. I had battled that myself, but as I got older I was able to overcome some of that. She never did. She was always happy for everyone else and genuinely thought they, whoever *they* were, deserved the best of everything, but not her.

She always felt guilty for moving away from the family farm. All of her siblings had married, moved away from the family farm, and had families. Nell had not. She somehow felt that, since she was single, it was her duty to stay on the farm and help her parents. She would rise every morning before five a.m. and help my grandfather milk the cows (they had a small dairy farm), then clean up and get ready for work.

The farm was about a twenty-minute drive from the public utility where she worked. She was the secretary to the manager and was completely dedicated to her job. She never called in sick and never stayed home due to snow or ice. She would put chains on her tires if necessary and make the twenty-minute trip.

Nell had graduated from a rural high school and would have loved to attend college, but that was out of the question for her, financially and geographically.

She had to immediately go to work since her parents struggled to get by on their small farm.

Fortunately, in the mid-1960's a community college opened in a nearby town. In her thirties, Nell decided to attend classes at night and get an associate's degree. I don't think anyone ever relished an educational opportunity as much as she did or benefited more from it.

Of course, she had to pay for it all herself, and she was still milking the cows at dawn, working all day, and then driving another forty-five minutes to attend classes. It wasn't easy at all for her, and it took her six years to get that degree, but it was life-changing.

I don't think she would have ever moved off the farm had she not gone to college. She was thirty-eight when she finally did get an apartment in town. Living in Boonetown, not too far from my home, Nell and I got to see more of each other, and she was able to come to more of the family dinners my mom and dad would have.

I always felt a connection with Nell. She loved the arts as much as did I. And, in a way, we were both loners. I understood her.

We had a bond.

Nell took me to see my first musical when I was around thirteen. It was the first production of our new community theater group, and I was just mesmerized: first of all, by how talented our local citizens were; and second, by the whole concept of the "musical." I had seen movie musicals and loved them, but I had never been to a live show. I fell in love with the art form.

A few years later, Nell bought us tickets to the

Tennessee Performing Arts Center Broadway series. I would drive Nell and myself to Nashville, and we would meet my sister for lunch and a show.

Nell looked forward to seeing those shows so much. She was stuck in a small town with limited cultural opportunities, but always made it to see any concerts or the symphony when they would come to town. She yearned to experience the arts and see more of the world. Even though her shyness was always something for her to overcome, she began to travel when the local bank organized a travel club. Being single always made traveling more expensive and a little more challenging for her, but she managed, and she loved it. Some people take the arts and vacations for granted. Not Nell. She relished every single moment.

Without a doubt though, the great love of her life was animals. Particularly cats. Having grown up on the farm, without a lot of other kids her own age around, I think animals were her friends and playmates.

One day, my sister was going over to check on Nell and spotted a woman climbing a ladder onto the roof of the house across the street. It was Nell. A stray cat was stranded on the roof, and when Nell saw it she immediately went into action. She was eighty-one at the time, but that wasn't going to stop her. If there was an animal in danger, Nell never paused for a second to think about her own safety.

There she was on the roof trying to get that cat safely down. Of course, Janice about had a heart attack, thinking of all the things Nell might break on the way down. But Nell would have never complained or blamed the cat if she ended up in traction.

The move to The Peak was good for Nell in every way, except one.

A year or so after her move there, a new resident had become infatuated with her and was trying to seduce her. Apparently, he had tried to get her to come to his room several times and at one point had tried to grope her. She had no interest in him. We thought at first that her sweet nature might have just been interpreted incorrectly. But we found out later that he was just very fond of women, and he was after all of them.

This groping incident brought out something that stunned us all, but wasn't entirely shocking to me either. While Nell was living at The Peak, my sister and I would bring her out to lunch with us one day every week. On one particular day, Janice said that on the way to lunch, Nell blurted out that she had been sexually harassed at work when she was younger. I won't go into the details, but from what my sister learned, it was way beyond some inappropriate flirtatious comments.

As I heard my sister tell it, some puzzle pieces seemed to fit into place.

After I graduated from college and began working at my father's company, I would meet Nell for lunch. We only worked a couple of blocks apart and I always liked to eat at the same diner she did, so it just was an easy fit. This went on from the time I was twenty-one until she moved to The Peak at age eighty-two. Pretty much every weekday, except vacations and holidays, we would meet for lunch and discuss the day's events. Over thirty years of lunches. Doing some quick math, I would say that we easily shared seven thousand or so meals.

I distinctly remember a period of time when she was suffering great anxiety about work. She never went into a lot of detail, but I could tell she was really scared to talk about it. Many days, she seemed almost distraught and was visibly upset at lunch. She would often speak of this one co-worker as a male chauvinist. She would talk about her disdain for him and how much she hated working with him. These were very strong words coming from her. She always got along with everyone.

I tried to help her, but didn't really know how. Looking back, I can see how she would have been an easy target for this type of abuse. She was attractive, single, and very shy. I think her abuser would have known that she would never go public. She also worked in an office in the back wing which was sort of removed from many of her co-workers, making unwanted "conversation" less likely to be overheard.

By the time she told us about this, my aunt did have some early dementia, but I had no doubt it really happened. We consulted with some social workers and had a therapist visit her for some counseling. Everyone we consulted agreed that even with early dementia, people don't come up with these types of memories randomly. The dementia may have let her barriers down enough to finally share this.

She brought it up again one day when she and I were at the deli having lunch with my friend Maggie. The look on her face said it all. The fear was still there. The anguish. The same look she had all those years ago when we had lunches together and it was actually occurring.

She said she knew no one would believe her, but it

really happened. I could see in her eyes that she had been waiting for years to have someone believe her and understand. Maggie was never at a loss for words, but at this moment she was quiet, leaving me stranded. I could only say to Nell that I believed her. And I did.

During this period, staff members at The Peak told us she had shared this story with them as well. Always the same. It broke my heart that I could not help her when it actually happened. I know she feared losing her job if she reported him, and I know he knew that too. This was at a time when women were often not believed, or were considered "too sensitive" or "too emotional" to work in a "man's world".

Not long after all these revelations "the groper" (as we called him) was moved out of The Peak due to his ongoing lewd behavior. My informant at The Peak had leaked the juicy details. Apparently, after the first groping incidents, he had been given a drug to *decrease* his sex drive. But according the staff member it wasn't strong enough, and he had to be shipped out because he continued to be a problem. I found out from another social worker that this is commonly done in nursing homes when a man can't seem to control his urges.

My nephew cracked me up when he asked if the drug was called "De-agra" or maybe "No-grope Dope."

After the offender left the facility, things returned to normal with my aunt and she never mentioned the incident at work again. I think seeing him and knowing him as a sexual predator brought all those memories back. After he left, thank God, those memories seemed to leave her.

Life got back to normal for a year or so, and then the COVID crisis hit. The facility had to be locked-down. For the next year, I would have to go to the back door of the building (which was right next to Nell's unit) and talk to her through the glass. I always told my friends that if you ever felt bad about yourself, you should go visit my aunt. She always made me feel special. She would tell me how much she appreciated my visit and that she knew how valuable my time was. She never wanted to keep me from my jobs.

She would always say that she knew my design reputation was spreading and I should get back to work. I'd always laugh and say well, manure spreads easily too, so I don't take my reputation too seriously. When my great niece began the first grade, Nell was convinced she would be her class president, and then the U.S. President someday. Or maybe a veterinarian, or a scientist.

Aunt Nell was always your biggest supporter.

She handled the lock-down pretty well, but I know she missed all the social interaction and activities she had become accustomed to. At least she could still see the staff many times a day. I cannot imagine how difficult COVID would have been for her had she still been living alone.

About two years into Nell's stay at The Peak, she got a bad urinary tract infection (UTI). As you may know, a UTI can be not only painful, but can also cause you to become quite wacky. Nell's dementia had been fairly stable since moving to The Peak, but an illness, or change of surroundings, could mess with that. Unfortunately, this UTI got bad before it was caught and she ended up in the hospital. She was never thirsty, so she would often get dehydrated too, so they ordered fluids and antibiotics. I was staying with her the night they gave her the fluids and things did not go well.

I had spent a very bad night in the hospital with my mother before she died of cancer when they gave her fluids—without a catheter—and that was a long night for sure. They said they would give my aunt a catheter since she was a fall risk. At first glance, this seemed like a great idea. No trips to the bathroom.

Wrong.

A UTI, a catheter, and dementia is truly a recipe for disaster.

I probably need to point out here that my aunt was a lifelong Democrat and proud of it. She had been quite distressed over the election of Donald Trump and would come out of her shell to state that. She would not call him President Trump, only Mr. Trump.

So here we were: me, Nell, the UTI, and the catheter, and it went like this. (After a while, I started writing down what she said. I knew that someday this would be really funny. It was not funny that night.)

Nell: "I need to go to the bathroom," as she starts crawling out of bed.

Me: "Nell, you have a catheter. Just stay in bed and relax. The catheter will collect the urine over here in this little bag." (Then I held up the bag for her to view.)

Nell: "Really? But I need to go to the bathroom."

Me: "I know, but you can go to the bathroom right there, just relax."

Nell: "When do I get to go to the bathroom?"

Me: "Well, you can't really, you are hooked up to this catheter and you can go whenever you need to right there."

Nell: "Who made up this rule?"

Me: "I think your doctor did."

Nell: "Do they do this in other states?"

Me: "Yes, I'm sure they do. Let me check with the nurses and see if we can get something to help you sleep."

Cut to me at the nurse's station begging for drugs. They respond saying they will call the doctor.

Back in the room:

Nell: "I need to go to the bathroom," as she again tries to crawl out of bed.

Me: "You have to stay in bed, you have a catheter."

Nell: "I'm an old-fashioned girl, I like to go to the bathroom the old-fashioned way."

Me: (Trying not to laugh) "I know, but tonight you have to use the catheter."

Nell: "I'm a country girl, we didn't do this on the farm."

Me: "I know, and I am really sorry you can't go to the bathroom, but you have a catheter."

Nell: "Who came up with this idea."

Me: "Your doctor."

Nell: "Can I go and pee outside?"

Me: "I'm sorry, you can't."

Meanwhile, I am wondering if they are ever going to bring something to help her sleep.

Nell: "Did they do this to you?"

Me: "No they didn't."

Nell: "Was this one of Mr. Trump's ideas?"

Me: (Trying not to die laughing) "Yes, I bet it was."

Nell: "This had to be one of Mr. Trump's ideas."

Me: "It might have been."

Nell: "Please impeach him already."

I'm laughing out loud at this point. It's been about three hours now and still no drugs and Nell is still trying to get up and go to the bathroom every few minutes. She cannot understand the catheter at all. Back at the nurse's station again, I am again begging for some sleeping meds. They finally say they have approval to give her some Benedryl. Well, I know that isn't going to help.

Back in the room:

Nell: "I need to go to the bathroom," as she tries to crawl out of bed.

Me: "You have to stay in bed, you have a catheter. They are coming to give you something to help you sleep."

Nell: "But I need to go to the bathroom."

Me: "You *are* going to the bathroom through the catheter."

Nell: "Is this a modern thing?"

Two hours have passed since the Benedryl and she isn't even a tiny bit sleepy. I am back at the nurse's station now doing my best Shirley McLaine imitation from *Terms of Endearment,* but things move very slowly in the middle of the night at a hospital. The nurse says she'll try to get something stronger.

Back in the room:

Nell: "This has got to be Mr. Trump's idea."

Me: "I agree."

Nell: "I think Mr. Trump is trying to change the way people pee."

That one killed me. I am dead.

Two more hours pass and it is five a.m. The nurse brings a sedative. Nell continues to try to get out of bed and go pee until about six a.m., when she finally dozes off. Within thirty minutes the nurses wake her up to check her vitals.

It was a long night.

One of my friends told me something her father said after he suffered a stroke. He had been a very successful business man and a leader in the community. After his stroke left him paralyzed, he said one day that, in the end, it didn't really matter what you had done or how successful you had been in life. It really all came down to dealing with your bodily functions. Sad, but oh, so true.

I've been very thankful that dementia never changed my aunt's sweet nature. I've heard of many cases where some very kind folks became very mean. But she was still the same sweetheart as always.

One day I was visiting her after the COVID restrictions had been lifted and vaccines were taken. I took a picture of her, as I often did, and could not help but be struck by her youthful look. At eighty-seven, not one wrinkle in her milky-white skin. Maybe some sagging around the jawline, but that was it. Her hair was still the auburn color of her youth, but with just some gray hair frosting the temples.

I think she was a testament to clean living. Nell never smoked or drank, and she exercised daily. She never, ever, had a suntan, much less a sunburn, and always wore hats and long sleeves when she mowed the yard. She used a generous amount of Noxema moisturizing creme every night at bedtime too. The staff at The Peak always talked about her flawless skin.

I took a picture that day because I kind of knew what was coming. I wanted to have a record of her still looking so young. Her dementia was advancing at a much faster pace. She was still there. Forgetful, but still there.

And still my biggest fan.

The one person that thought I could do no wrong. Someone who would have fought for me. Her kindness was still in-tact. Her love of animals still epic. And, above all, she was still humble. Humble as she has always been.

But things changed quickly. I knew that Nell's quality time was over and done. We were down to the bad days. I began to want less time for her, not more. Less suffering, less fear, less confusion.

One Friday, as they tried to feed her lunch, her breathing suddenly went haywire, and the family was called in. We were thankful hospice got there quickly to keep her comfortable. She died later that day, surrounded by her favorite people. It was autumn, and autumn was her favorite season. A broken hip turned out to be the final blow and it sent her dementia to the final stage.

I went to Nashville the next day to find her an outfit for her burial. She wanted a traditional Catholic funeral, and we followed through with that request. I had been her personal shopper for so many years and always helped her pick out her clothes. It felt right that I would buy a nice fall-colored sweater set. She loved sweaters and this set complemented her auburn hair. I knew she would love it.

Now, I feel nothing but gratitude. Thankful that her suffering is over. Grateful for all the years we had, for all those thousands of lunches we shared, and all the quality time.

She remains the kindest and most humble person I've ever known. Always putting others first, herself last. Never feeling she deserved to be loved and yet loved by everyone she met.

Godspeed.

MY STYLE

I love fashion. It kind of fits with my love of interior design. I like to see things presented in their best light. I love good proportions, good fit, and most of all good style.

I love it to the point that it can be very distracting to me.

On the television show *The Golden Girls*, the girls had to pool their money to have the roof leak repaired or the plumbing fixed, and yet they all had extensive wardrobes. They had new cocktail dresses and evening gowns for every charity ball they organized or attended—and they did a lot of those. They also could afford very elaborate costumes for every dress-up occasion.

It just bugged me. Yes, I know these are fictional television characters, but, still, it just isn't very realistic.

Of course, fashion isn't handled realistically in the movies either.

In the classic film *The Sound of Music*, we are asked to believe that the young novice nun, played by the fabulous Julie Andrews, made two-piece play outfits out of curtains for seven children—overnight. That's right, I said seven. I couldn't even focus on her singing ability for thinking about her kick-ass sewing skills.

She used the curtains from her bedroom since they didn't have play clothes, and that is plausible. The fact that they all fit perfectly—and she could not have had patterns on hand—was, on the other hand, astounding.

What was really unbelievable was the wardrobe she created for herself. If you recall, Maria had given all her clothes to the poor when she entered the abbey. Then when she came from the abbey to the VonTrapp home, she had only one plain dress. So, when she told the captain she could sew, he had fabrics sent to her— three or four different bolts of fabric, it appeared—so she could make her own clothes.

Julie—I mean Maria—proceeded to create a couture collection of perfectly fitted day-dresses with ridiculous amounts of detail work. They had fitted bodices with matching belts and blouses, and one even had smocking at the neckline and waist. Any one of these outfits would take many hours to make, and yet she—while taking care of seven children— had a beautiful new outfit every day. None of the contestants on *Project Runway* have a thing on her. In my opinion, her skills were not best used for teaching children to sing. She should have started a fashion line.

Of course, fashion and style are not the same thing. Fashion is something you can buy and own. Style is something you simply possess. You either have it or you don't. Wearing the latest fashion can get you noticed, in a good—or sometimes a bad—way. But if you have *style*, it always shows—even on a bad day. It's the way you wear your clothes and the way they

My Style

fit, the way you personalize an outfit and how you flip a collar. It's just there, and it shows.

I love to see someone who has developed their own style and really owns it. I have some friends who have great personal style. The common denominator is that none of them follow trends or wear faddish clothes. They know what works for them and they don't stray from that formula.

One person whose style developed into fashion icon status during her lifetime was Princess Diana. We are almost the same age, so I was always very aware of her. I had never been interested in the royal family before her, but something about her drew me in.

Part of it was watching her fashion evolution. I watched her style develop over the years and I know it well. Even all these years after her death, with all the photos and video of her, they still never get her look right in film portrayals.

Like on the *Netflix* series *The Crown*, when Diana wore the famous black cocktail *revenge dress*. I saw a promotional photo recently, and they got the dress right, but they used a tacky four-strand pearl choker with a small sapphire broach. It was supposed to look like the big sapphire broach and seven-strand choker Diana had crafted for herself.

It did not.

It was so cheap looking.

Diana was gifted the enormous broach (the sapphire was the size of a small egg) by the Queen when she married, but it always looked boring and stuffy as a broach. I never liked it. I don't think she did either.

Several years later, she had the broach crafted into the

center clasp of a choker with seven strands of tiny pearls supporting it. Diana loved pearl chokers and wore a variety of them. This necklace became a signature piece for her and by far her most formal piece of jewelry—other than her tiaras. I would guess it was one of Diana's favorite pieces of jewelry—she wore it a lot. It was my favorite of hers too.

The choker on *The Crown* was all wrong. In fact, I would never be able to tell you a thing about how good the scene was because, after I saw the cheap choker, they lost me.

I thought the necklace was such an apt metaphor for Diana's life in the royal family. The broach was very formal and stuffy, yet when she added all the pearls it made it less so. She gave it the softer, more-approachable touch she was known for.

The night that Diana died in a car crash in Paris, I had gotten home very late and just happened to turn on the television and saw the news. Just a few minutes later, they announced she had died. I was incredibly sad. Mostly for her two sons. But also because I knew I would miss her presence in the world.

She had finally come into her own, I thought: a sleek, more-confident version of the young girl who first took the stage in a gigantic royal wedding. In the days after her death, seeing her humanity and compassion being shared in countless stories on television only reinforced my feelings for her. She was somehow able to humanize a cold, old-fashioned monarchy that desperately needed some fresh blood. She had made headlines with all of her charitable work. Her simple acts of human kindness endeared

My Style

her to the world, like her refusal to wear gloves when visiting AIDS patients after being advised strongly by the monarchy to do so.

In that one moment, she changed the way people worldwide viewed AIDS patients, and filled a much-needed role for them as an ambassador of hope. She was always willing to reach out to those who were in need or suffering. It was something we had never seen from the stuffy monarchy and, unsurprisingly, her popularity eclipsed theirs in a short time.

It's easy to see why. Most images showed Diana walking toward the crowds with a warm smile and outstretched arms, ready to give a stranger a hug. The queen and prince did all their walking down the center of the street barely making eye contact, never touching anyone. It became obvious—in a strange twist of fate—that she had simply outgrown them.

It's so ironic, looking back on it all. They were so worried she might not be up to their standards, yet she created a new standard for behavior among the royals. Her charisma was too much for them to contain. I think it took her longer to see her own power, but the world saw it right away. That power began to show in her wardrobe too. Her style was evolving.

Gone were the loose-fitting floral dresses with lace collars and lots of trim. The princess-y evening gowns with big "poof" skirts made an exit as well. She was only nineteen when thrust into that royal world, and she (understandably) dressed like a young girl in the early years. As Diana matured, she found new designers like Catherine Walker, who helped her re-shape her silhouette into a sleeker, more streamlined version of herself. Her day attire was now two-piece fitted suits, suitable for a working woman, or simple body-hugging shift dresses.

The heels were now higher and usually Jimmy Choo's. Diana was wearing Jimmy Choo's before he became a household name. Her fantastic figure and long legs were now on display. Her formal wear transitioned to long, slim, navy or black tank-style dresses. She would often pair them with the sapphire and pearl choker. The hair got shorter and more carefree too. Her confidence was showing, and her new, more-casual, modern wardrobe only added to that confidence.

She always seemed to pull out some of her best looks here in the USA. I think of the ink-blue Victor Edelstein gown she famously danced in at the White House, or the deep-blue, Catherine Walker tank-style dress she wore with slicked-down hair and the sapphire choker as she presented Liz Tiberis a fashion award in New York. Both were great looks for her.

For me, though, it was in Chicago that she was her most confident and stunning, in the simple, purple Versace gown with pearl and amethyst accessories. Near the end of her life, she had found bold, sleek looks from Versace, and had begun to wear his designs often. And after a life of being on the public stage, she finally seemed to be totally at ease and her most beautiful. This was not long before her tragic death.

When I see images of her on TV or the internet today, I often wonder what she would be doing today. I think she would be living here in the USA, and I can only imagine the good work she might have done in the last twenty years. And she would have been doing those good works in great style, I'm sure. I miss her.

I have been shopping with, and have helped dress, a lot of women over the years. Well, not technically put them *in* the clothes, but advised them and put their look together. Now, what's out there in the stores is all over the place. I don't see a lot of clothes that flatter women. It's kind of sad. Especially for women of a certain age. There just aren't things out there for a woman who still wants to wear tailored well-made clothes. I think this is why I don't see as many women these days with great style.

The best piece of advice I can give to women—and to men too for that matter—is to make sure your clothes fit well. If the clothes don't fit properly, it doesn't matter how expensive or how fashionable they are, you won't look good. This applies to every body-size and type—women or men.

At least women can have more fun with fashion. Bags, jewelry, scarves… all can add so much to a look. Women just have so many more options.

I was in Miami a few years ago at an outdoor shopping center. It was warm out, and I thought it was rather odd that a woman had a yellow scarf wrapped around her neck and shoulders several times. I was walking behind her and, since I walk very fast, I was approaching her rather quickly. When I got about five feet from her, I saw the yellow scarf raise up and look at me. After I jumped back about ten feet and began to breathe again, I realized that it was a huge yellow boa-constrictor casually draped about her. She acted like it was no big deal, and I could tell she kind of got off on the shock value.

Even more shocking to me was encountering two more women, out shopping at that same plaza, with snakes wrapped around them. I supposed they were all either trying to give their pets some fresh air, or were *really* into reptile accessories. Is this a Miami thing? I have no idea, but it put me on edge the entire day. I think they should have some sort of warning placard or at least a snake-lane for people sporting snakes.

Keep in mind, I am the first to recommend a reptile fashion accessory, but I am usually referring to a bag, or maybe shoes. Trust me when I say, a live snake is *not* what I had in mind. I'm pretty much of the mindset that none of your fashion accessories should be alive.

The only person that really pulled that off was Audrey Hepburn in the movie *Sabrina*. When she arrived back in the U.S. from Paris and was wearing a perfectly tailored Givenchy suit, walking a well-coiffed poodle at her side. That worked. Her entire wardrobe from that movie worked.

I know a lot of people think fashion is superficial, that it's just something for people that have too much expendable income and are too focused on their appearance. And I guess that might be true.

But when I am wearing clothes that I know fit well, look good, and put me in my best light, I feel great. It makes me a little more confident and more relaxed. I'd like to be that person that can walk into a room wearing *anything* and feel great about themselves, but I am not. I am aware of how often we are being judged on our appearance.

I think part of it, for me, was formed in my childhood.

I was never able to find clothes to fit my tall and skinny frame. My sleeves were always too short, as were my pants. It drove me crazy. I wanted to be able to walk into a store and buy clothes—that fit— off the rack, like everyone else. I wanted nice clothes. I just could never find them.

As I got older, I did find some brands that I could wear and places to order tall sizes, but the choices were always limited and not very stylish. For years, I wondered if that's why I was so interested in clothes. It does seem that you always want what you *can't* have.

But who am I kidding? I simply love clothes. Always have, always will. Maybe it's the designer in me.

And to prove that point, now that I *can* find more things in my size it hasn't made me want them any less. And even though I have many more options in clothing these days, I still seldom find the *really* cool things I want in my size—that elusiveness makes me appreciate it even more when I find something special that fits.

Over the years, I have managed to accumulate a nice wardrobe. It has probably taken me about ten times as long as an average-sized person, but that's ok too. I kind of like the hunt. I guess I'll always spend a little too much time worrying about what I'm going to wear because I do want to make a good impression. And I kind of hope I always feel that way.

That's just my style.

TRIALS AND TRIBULATIONS

This was not the trial of the century. Not even the trial of the month. The courtroom was not packed. There were no cameras. No one really cared.

Except us: me, my brother, and the Miltons.

It was a silly lawsuit in my opinion. Mr. Milton was a former employee we had terminated because he would not work out-of-town.

We were in the midst of the economic crash of 2007 and 2008. The only electrical jobs we had going were out-of-town. Many of our competitors had completely shut down due to loss of work, and we were trying to stay afloat. New construction was completely dead at that time, but we were lucky to have some long-term customers who continued to need maintenance work. These customers were not local.

So it was pretty simple. Mr. Milton was an electrician. If he wanted to keep his job, he would have to travel and work out-of-town during the week and come home every weekend. Just like all the other electricians were doing.

Milton's argument was that his wife was in poor health, and that he had to be home every night to check on her. We sympathized with him, but all of our employees wanted to be home with their wives and families every night too. We just did not have any local work for Mr. Milton, or any of the others.

I wasn't happy about the situation. I didn't like to have to let anyone go. But I was worried about the future of the entire company. My main concern was the one hundred other employees we had, who were grateful to have work *anywhere*. Mr. Milton was not going to get special treatment.

So, we gave him the choice. And he once again refused to travel. He was terminated.

But it turned out not to be so simple. He sued us.

Our insurance company was scheduled to defend us, but they were not doing that job very well. They had changed the attorney on our case the day before the trial, and he was completely unprepared. What he found out, as he read up on the case, was that the Miltons planned to use Mrs. Milton's illnesses as the basis for the lawsuit. We weren't sure how, but it seemed that the whole case would be a sympathy plea to the judge.

It was.

The only witnesses on their side were Mr. and Mrs. Milton. (I call them Mr. and Mrs. because they were my elders, and I was taught to address my elders that way as a child.) He was already past retirement age, but wanted to keep working. I felt sure they would try to use age discrimination as the basis of the lawsuit. I was really shocked that this was never mentioned, though. I am not sure how old Mrs. Milton was. Her makeup was too thick to tell, but I would say mid-to-late-sixties.

We only met this attorney moments before the trial.

My brother was seated next to our new attorney. I was sitting right behind my brother. (I just had a feeling I would need someone to hide behind.)

In the opening statement, we learned of our supposed "cruel and inhumane treatment of Mr. Milton": how we had demanded he travel, which would endanger the health of his wife. We also learned (according to their attorney) that we had plenty of local work, but we tried to force Mr. Milton to leave town for literally months at a time—just because we were mean, I guess. We were some sorry sons-of-bitches, according to this man.

Their first witness was Mr. Milton, who testified, under oath, that he absolutely had to be home every night to give his wife "her pill". The lawyer said, "Now Mr. Milton, would you explain to the court what will happen to Mrs. Milton if you don't get home every night and give her this pill?"

"She will die," Mr. Milton said, "I have to be there to give it to her every night or she will die."

Wow. I thought, *That must be one hell of a pill.*

Mr. Milton went on to testify that we were just picking on him, that we had other employees working locally, and that he should be able to choose where he wanted to work. (The other employees he was referring to *were not* electricians.) I caught the judge rolling her eyes a bit at that statement. Mr. Milton was asking for his job back, or a nice cash settlement for the pain and suffering we had caused him. (We had done some research before the trial and were not shocked to find out he had sued a number of other employers in the past.)

When Mrs. Milton took the stand, it was a dramatic

moment. I was expecting her to arrive on a gurney, or at least in a wheel chair, but no, she walked right up to the stand with only a cane for assistance and took a seat.

She was heavily made-up, with jet-black hair that was obviously dyed and teased-up high, and she was wearing a lot of jewels. She looked a lot like an older Liz Taylor in one of the *White Diamonds* commercials.

Their lawyer spoke to her very softly, as if she were so delicate that a loud noise might stop her heart. Not too long into the questioning, the lawyer was almost crying. He seemed truly upset about having to be bothering someone in her fragile state.

Then, quietly and gently, he asked, "Mrs. Milton, how's your health?"

Mrs. Milton uttered a long-slow-mournful "Not good," just loud enough for the judge to hear. She said, "I have cholesterol, blood pressure, a hiatal hernia, sciatica, rheumatism, and diverticulitis.

"Oh, I'm so sorry. That must be so painful for you," the lawyer said.

"It is," she managed to utter in reply, as a tear rolled down her rouged cheek.

The lawyer apologized again for having to bother her with such invasive questions and patted her on the hand as if preparing her for the worst. Then he said, "Could you tell us how Mr. Milton's termination has affected your *home* life."

"Well, that's not good either," she said. "Ever since he was terminated, he hasn't been able to perform his husbandly duties."

"Awe, I'm sorry" the Lawyer said, again about to sob.

"That must be very difficult for you."

Mrs. Milton, who was wiping tears by this time, said, "Yes, it is very difficult."

I was amazed that she even wanted any of her husband's husbandly duties, considering the laundry list of ailments she had given. But they were pulling out all the stops. I hear that "loss of affection" always gets sympathy from a jury.

There was no jury here, however. It was up to the judge.

The judge was a lady in her late fifties, I think, and seemed to be a kind of no-nonsense gal. It was very hard to get a read on her, but I did sense, at times, that she was rather put out by this entire trial.

"And, Mrs. Milton," the lawyer said as he began his final gut-wrenching question, "would you please tell the court what will happen if your husband isn't home every night to see that you take your pill."

"I'll die," she said bluntly.

"Your honor, I rest my case." The lawyer said with all the dramatic flair he could muster.

I'd like to say you could have heard a pin drop in the courtroom when he closed his arguments, but since my brother was literally vibrating in his seat, that wasn't completely true.

I wanted to be irate, and I felt I deserved to be, but this was just so damn funny. I was doing everything possible not to laugh. I didn't want the judge to see me laughing. Although, I got the feeling she wanted to laugh a few times herself.

When our lawyer cross-examined Mr. Milton, my brother and I both whispered to him, "Ask him where he lives."

We thought our attorney never would, but finally he did ask him that question and found out that Mr. Milton lived a good hour-drive away from Boonetown, and was traveling that far every day to work and back home. So, technically, he was working out-of-town every day. He continued questioning and found out from Mr. Milton that his wife was at home, alone, for at least eleven to twelve hours a day and able to take care of herself.

Mr. Milton said, "That doesn't matter at all! If I am out of town in the evening, she might forget to take her pill at night, and then she would die."

I was thinking a simple phone call every night to remind her to take this life-saving tablet might work the same way, but apparently that was simply not an option. He had to be there to give it to her himself, as he reiterated a number of times.

The judge and my brother and I were all dying of curiosity about "the pill."

We knew it was too late for birth-control, and we all wanted to know what was in that magic capsule and what it was treating. It is one of the great mysteries of my life that our attorney never asked him to explain the contents of the pill. We certainly prodded him to do so.

I must say that Mr. and Mrs. Milton were good witnesses. I think they had prepared a great deal at home and they both took it quite seriously. The judge dismissed us and said we would receive a written ruling in a week or so.

We have never had any luck in court cases. Thankfully, we've never been in any major litigation, but the other few occasions where we were involved in a lawsuit, it didn't go our way. This time, though, I just could not imagine any way that the judge could rule in his favor.

During this same economic recession, another employee situation came to a head. This was one of those times when anyone would really hate being in charge of the family business. But there I was, and the economy was still tanking.

Harry was a long-time employee and a long-time problem. He had been with us for years and years and, although a very likable fellow, he had become our worst worker.

My dad always felt a sense of loyalty to his employees, and I do too, as long as that loyalty works both ways. Dad hated firing anyone, especially someone that had been with us so long.

Dad felt sorry for Harry, I think, since he had a family to support. But, we could no longer afford to keep a non-productive person on board. He was blatantly breaking company policy: missing work, always late, and not getting his work done. It was time to let him go.

I decided that I would go ahead and clean out his office the night before I let him go. That way, we didn't have to have that awkward clean-out-your-desk time *after* he had gotten the bad news. I knew he was expecting it. Honestly, I really think he was hoping to be let go so he could just goof-off full-time. Goofing-off certainly was his go-to activity at work.

While I was cleaning out his desk, I found a bag full of drug paraphernalia—pipes and such, and some pot. *Well, this is interesting*, I thought. I knew he drank. I was pretty sure I could smell liquor on his breath after he returned *late* from lunch. But I never knew of him doing drugs. His kids did, though. He had told me that.

His kids were in their late teens and early twenties at that time, and both were still living at home. Harry told me that they had become such a problem during high school—drinking and smoking pot late into the night—that he had hooked up a camper-trailer in his back yard for them to live in, so they would not disturb his sleep. This seemed like a good solution for Harry, but it occurred to me that he was probably not in the running for parent-of-the-year.

He had never been able to say no to his kids. I had been around him all my life and I had seen him give-in to them time and time again. According to Harry, everything that went wrong for them was the teacher's fault or someone else's fault. So now they were adults without employment and no desire to even look for jobs.

Finding the drugs in his desk did sort of streamline things a bit. Since we had a "no drugs" policy at work, I would use this as the primary reason for termination and not have to go into the laundry-list of other issues. But when I told him we would be terminating his employment due to his possession of drugs, he was quick to offer an explanation.

He said that the drugs were not his, so I could not fire him on that basis. I inquired, "Well, whose are they?"

To which he replied, "They are my boys' drugs."

I was not surprised that they were his boys' drugs, but I was shocked that he would admit this.

He went on to explain "I was having my boys' truck

cleaned and detailed for them," (a truck which Harry was making payments for), "and I knew the guy that was cleaning the truck would steal their drugs. And, if he stole their drugs, I would have to buy them more drugs, so I figured the best thing to do was to hide the drugs in my desk while the truck was being cleaned."

So was it just an accident that they happened to be in his desk on the day I fired him? Is he really thinking this is a logical excuse? Harry continued to protest, saying since they were not his drugs, this was definitely not grounds for firing him.

I was sort of in shock when that explanation was laid out. My only response to Harry was, "Do you know how many things are wrong with that excuse?" He didn't get what I meant. In his head, this was a legitimate excuse. When it came to his boys, he was completely blind.

I don't think it occurred to him that I might find it odd that, first of all, he was having a truck cleaned and detailed for two young unemployed men, loaded with free time. Or second, that he was willing to buy them drugs in the first place, or third, willing to buy them more drugs in case those were stolen.

There was more back and forth and then I finally said, "The ownership of the drugs really doesn't matter here. Having the drugs in your possession is violation of company policy and it is grounds for termination, so we are letting you go."

About that time, my dad, who still came to the office daily, walked by.

I was hoping to avoid this very thing. My dad was so soft-hearted, and I was afraid if Harry made a tearful appeal Dad might cave-in and try to overrule me.

And, just as I feared, Harry did approach my dad and brought him into the discussion.

Harry said—and this is a direct quote—a line I will never, ever forget, "Mr. Evers, did y'all really fire me 'cause of them drugs, or was it just 'cause I ain't worth a shit?"

My dad thought a moment and said, "Harry, do you really want me to answer that?"

Harry got up, said, "I guess not," and left.

We never saw him in the office again, and to my knowledge he never held down another job in his life. He was probably around fifty when we let him go. His wife worked, I believe, and I guess that kept him going. So I think really, in the end, he got exactly what he wanted.

Mr. and Mrs. Milton, thank goodness, did not get exactly what they wanted.

Just as promised, the judge mailed the decision out a week later and pretty much went down the list of arguments, saying none of them were valid or made sense. She saw everything exactly as we did and ruled in our favor.

My faith in the justice system was restored.

ODE TO SAVANNAH

I'll go ahead and tell you now that if you are looking for any romance in my stories, this is going to be it.
I fell madly in love with Savannah.
The city.
The book *Midnight in the Garden of Good and Evil* was a huge hit in the 1990s and stayed on the best seller list for years. I don't think I read it until a couple of years after it came out, but I loved it. It was full of the type of small-town, southern characters that I love to write about.

Jon Berendt, the author, was visiting Savannah when a murder occurred in the most famous and beautiful house in town—lucky break for him—so he stayed in Savannah through all four of the ensuing trials. Jim Williams (the accused) was pretty famous himself in Savannah, and he became even more famous while enduring all the trials. He was ultimately acquitted.

It was a great true-crime story, and I do *love* true-crime stories.

At first, *Midnight in the Garden of Good and Evil* intrigued me because of the subject matter. Then, when I sat down to read it, something else got my attention.

The author went into great detail about the city of Savannah. I guess I had heard of Savannah—like in *Gone with the Wind*. But I had never really read a description like the one in the book. It sounded so beautiful. And very unique. The more I read, the more I became fascinated with Savannah.

I began to look-up pictures online so I could see the places he was speaking of, and they were just as beautiful as he painted them to be. It didn't take me long to decide that I needed to explore it for myself. So, I did.

Andy (a friend of mine from my college days who also appreciated old southern cities) and I headed over to check it out.

Savannah isn't easy to get to from Tennessee...or anywhere. You basically have to drive to Atlanta to start, and then you proceed south through Macon, and from there it's about two-and-a-half very-boring hours of nothing but pine trees and pavement.

But as soon as we exited Interstate-16, into the downtown historic district, I knew this place was different. It was the first time I had been on an interstate when the road just *ran out*. Of course, we were not far from the coast, so it had to end. But it was as if the interstate was just dropping us off at our destination: downtown Savannah. There was nowhere else to go.

Once you enter downtown Savannah, you are embraced by all the live oak trees with moss dripping down from the limbs. They form arches over the streets and it feels like you are in a kind of dreamy forest. At night, everything has a hazy quality about it.

Down the center medians, there are hundreds, maybe thousands of azaleas, and there's lush landscape everywhere you look. Stylish row houses line the streets, mixed in between schools and churches and municipal buildings. I could not wait to get checked-in at the hotel and start exploring Savannah on foot.

Everything Jon Berendt had said was true. It was stunning.

I really didn't have much interest in talking to the locals about the book. I just wanted to soak in all of the city. Well, actually, just the historic district. The rest of the city was ok, but it could have been most anywhere. It was the historic district that was truly unique. There were twenty-one city squares, in a grid pattern, with divided streets breaking up the pattern. It was designed specifically to prevent people from moving quickly through town. The concept was to stroll and enjoy the beauty—not just speed through. It was a brilliant concept that worked then and is still working today, a few hundred years later.

Each square has its own look, with some sort of monument and unique landscape design in the center park. Most squares have a dominant style of architecture. The squares closest to the coast have simpler homes in a colonial style, but as you progress further into town the houses and buildings become more and more ornate and grand. It was fascinating to walk from one square to the next and watch the progression.

I couldn't get enough of the place. I went back several times in the next couple of years.

On that first trip (and many more to follow) everywhere we went, people were talking about

Midnight in the Garden of Good and Evil. The tourists wanted to meet all the characters in the book, since they were all real and many of them still lived there.

It wasn't hard to tell that the locals had two very distinct views about what they simply referred to as "the book." A lot of locals loved "the book". They found a multitude of ways to profit from its success and from the huge boost in tourism it brought. Some started tour services, some opened up gift shops, and some of the people who had gained fame from being mentioned in the book opened up restaurants or night clubs and performed. Those venues were themed with the book in mind, geared to milk as much money out of tourists as possible.

The other faction of residents was not at all happy about the book. Many of them had lived in Savannah all their lives and felt it was beneath them. They did not want to be part of profiting off of an embarrassing crime. They also hated all the tourism and crowds the book brought. They were perfectly content with old Savannah. Of course, they also knew that much of the restoration of some of the downtown landmarks would have never happened without all the tourism, but they surely didn't want to admit it. They did not want or need—in their opinion—the help.

Over the years of visiting, I began to understand that. Sure, on our first visit, Andy and I went to that little night club above The Pirates' House to see the Lady-of-One-Thousand-Songs. She was featured in the book and we thought it might be fun.

She had gotten a little older by this time and had to be rolled over to the piano in a wheel chair, but managed to take requests from the audience for over an hour and no one stumped her. It was quite entertaining, I must say.

On that first trip, we also took in a lot of the other sights talked about in the book. But after that, I was ready to move on. I was over the book and those characters.

The town, however, was not over it and would not be for a decade or two. The problem with the book is that it was a double-edged sword. Had I not read it, I might not have discovered Savannah for many more years. I hated to admit to the locals that the book was what had originally brought me there. It made me feel so very ordinary. Those other book-readers simply could not feel the same connection to this city that I felt—at least that's what I wanted to believe.

I liked that it wasn't perfect. Parts of the downtown were still a bit gritty, and I liked that. I especially loved that there were no chain restaurants or chain stores in the downtown when I first started visiting. Every place was unique. But as the crowds came, that began to change. It took a while, I guess a couple of decades maybe, but now downtown has lots of chain eateries and expensive chain retail establishments.

Over the years, Savannah has continued to feed my creative soul. I love all the art galleries in the historic district, and I have gotten to know a lot of the artists. It is so nice to stop in and catch up with them when I make a trip. They give me the intel on the new restaurants and anything else I should check out. I bought so many wonderful paintings there over the years. It's obvious why the art there is so great: there is simply so much inspiration. Everywhere you look there is a scene worthy of being captured.

There were times when I went to Savannah simply because it was spring, or because of an event. There were also times when I went because I needed to go. I needed to get away, to escape to the place where I could always relax and always feel comforted. If something wasn't going well, I knew Savannah would make me feel better. It always did. There was a healing quality I felt when I would spend a day walking the squares and studying the latest improvements to the historic buildings. My legs might be tired from walking the uneven stone sidewalks, but my mind would be clear.

In early 2003, my mother was almost three years into her battle against cancer. She had been through many ups and downs since her diagnosis, but the treatments were beginning to fail her and the options were more and more limited. I had gone to Savannah several times during her illness and it always helped me to regroup from the cancer battle, if only for a few days.

I felt like we were heading into the final phase of her illness, but she was stable at the moment, and I thought a quick trip to my favorite place might help me prepare for the inevitable.

On that long drive to Savannah, I thought about so many things. One thought that kind of stuck in my brain was how I could spend so much time with my mom and still not know some simple things about her.

I knew who her favorite people were and what kind of clothes and foods she liked, but I didn't know a lot of little things like what her favorite song was, or her favorite city, or her favorite flower. I wished she had shared more of her thoughts with me. I wish she had told me the story of how she and my dad met. I think I know, but I never heard her tell it. She was never one to share her feelings freely.

I do remember once she said she liked the song *Send in the Clowns*, and she even asked my sister to buy her a copy of it. It might have been her favorite, but she never said it was. I thought that was such an odd choice. I really couldn't see why she would connect with that particular song. But she had never—to my knowledge—asked anyone to buy a record for her, so I figured she must have really liked it.

I also thought about her initial diagnosis and first chemotherapy treatments. She was never vain, but I could tell that the prospect of losing her hair was really bothering her. She had nice, thick, auburn hair. When she started her first round of chemo, I went to a wig shop in Nashville with her photos. I asked the clerk to order a wig in her hair color and to cut and style it like my mother's hair. She did, and I had it on hand when the inevitable day arrived.

She told me that her hair had begun to come out in clumps and that she had been putting-off washing it, fearing the rest would follow. She could wait no longer, though, and finally washed her hair. I went out to her house for moral support and took my hair clippers along. I have seen cancer victims with a splotchy scalp of bare patches and hanging shreds of hair, and to me that looks much sadder than being bald. I certainly didn't want her to look like that, or to have to trim it off herself. I wanted to be able to take care of that for her.

I didn't know how she would feel, or what it would look like, but when she finished shampooing, hair was everywhere in the bathroom. Her scalp was mostly bare, with some random patches of hair remaining. I told her not to look into the mirror while I trimmed it up.

She didn't.

I joked about how, now, she would know what I felt like. Then, I fit the wig on her head and asked her to go in the other room while I cleaned up.

After she left the room, I almost lost it. Cleaning up wet hair is always a nasty job, but when it's this kind of omen, it's more than just a messy clean-up. I figured Mom would want to take off the wig and look at herself in private, so I left after Dad got home.

She made it through that first round of chemo without many side effects, and we were hopeful it would do the trick, but within six months, the cancer was back—in her brain.

This time, radiation killed the tumors on her brain and, again, she had pretty-good days for several months. Her hair came back after the brain radiation and, even though it was a new color and texture, she was happy to have it.

Then it became a cat and mouse game—watching the numbers. Trying one chemo until it became ineffective and then trying another. We were on chemo number four when I went to Savannah.

I had only stayed three nights. On my last night there I decided to go to *The Olde Pink House* for dinner and eat down in the tavern. I love that restaurant and I love to eat in that cozy old space. There is a piano there, and a man usually plays show tunes while you dine. He had been playing the Gershwin's, Cole Porter, and Rogers and Hammerstein—classic show tunes—for most of the evening.

Then, as I was about to finish my meal, he played Sondheim. He hadn't played a living composer all evening and then he played Stephen Sondheim's *Send in the Clowns*. The one song that I *knew* my mom liked. It was like a sudden jolt back to reality.

On any other trip, it might have brought back a pleasant memory of her, but on this trip, I knew it meant something different. We had been waiting on her latest bloodwork, and this song, at this moment, somehow let me know it would not be good. The next morning as I was preparing to leave, my sister called to tell me what I already knew.

Even Savannah could not take my mind from this battle with cancer—my mother's battle that also felt like my own. All the way home, I thought about her: the thousands of home-cooked meals, the attempts to fit me with clothing, her constant presence in my life, and the rock she had always been for the family. All during cancer she still remained tough, never complaining and never seeking sympathy. Mostly though, I thought about how grateful I was for the many years we had spent as mother and son. It was the time I needed to face what lie ahead.

Within a few months, she was gone.

After her death, I would return to Savannah time and again. It is still the one place that I can actually relax. And each and every time I return there, even after her death, I instinctively pick up my phone to let my mom know I have arrived safely. It is always a little bit of a sad shock when I remember she isn't there to call.

I began to toy with the idea of buying a place in Savannah. Prices in the historic district were constantly on the rise and I felt like, if I wanted to spend some of my retirement time there, now might be the time to purchase. I thought I could rent it out when I wasn't using it and maybe even make some money on it. I told myself this and tried to make it have some sort of logic. But deep down, I just wanted to be able to lay claim to a little piece of this city I loved so much.

I made an offer on a unit in a historic building on Lafayette Square. It was small, but the two-room condo had high ceilings and the building was dripping with character. I felt the price I paid was actually good, considering the location was beyond prime. It was right in the center of the historic district, on one of the prettiest squares. I really could not believe it.

There were the typical realities to deal with. I had purchased in a building with more nit-picky rules that one could imagine. It seemed that all the older residents felt they needed to enforce all these rules as well. Residents were constantly being watched. Especially by the woman who walked her poodle in a frilly, lace-covered baby carriage.

I thought she had a grandchild for the longest time, until I passed by her closely on the sidewalk one day, allowing me to see the elderly poodle. There was a large hook on the carriage that she (only on certain days) attached a birdcage to. Her parrot would then tag along for the ride.

It wasn't until after I had owned that unit for several months that I realized that my building was actually in the book. Early in the book, a man, I believe named Joe Odom, had bought an old telephone exchange building and was converting it to condominiums. He talked sweet, southern widows into making deposits on units in the building, but ended up skipping out with the money and never coming through with the condos. The building went into bankruptcy after that and then eventually the bank sold off the units. I think my unit had been through two owners, one after the selloff and one before my purchase, but I am not sure.

I do know that I loved that condo and I loved the feeling of owning a tiny part of that city.

I did not, however, love the drive. It got to be exhausting. Definitely too far for a long weekend. Basically, a full day of driving each way. If you got lucky—really lucky—you might make it in eight hours, but if there were traffic issues, it could take nine or even ten. After several years, it began to feel like a burden. I was afraid it was taking away some of the pleasure I got from Savannah. Feeling that I must go to check on the condo, rather than going because I wanted to. I decided to sell. I hated to let it go, and sometimes I regret it, but I know it was the right decision.

It only took a couple of years after I sold the unit for the itch to return, and I, of course, began to visit Savannah again. Not nearly as often, but how could I not? We had a connection.

It's a different city now than when I first discovered it. It is definitely more crowded. Thousands and thousands of tourists flock there, and I cannot blame them.

It is still totally unique, though. The design of the downtown historic district is one that will never be repeated anywhere. It can't be. Modern zoning laws would never allow this combination of public and private spaces to co-exist so closely, and a modern government would never have the funds to build and maintain twenty-one public squares in another city.

Making the journey to Savannah less often has made it feel more special when I do visit. Its breathtaking beauty has a stronger punch when you haven't witnessed it in a while.

And just knowing Savannah is always there, waiting for my return—ready to inspire—makes me happy indeed.

THE FLAT TIRE

It was Christmas Day, 1991. I know this was the date because I just looked it up. It was the day the movie *The Prince of Tides* opened. I remember this because my friend Sarah called me that Christmas and asked me if I wanted to go see the movie. All of her Christmas activities were over and so were mine—I had nothing going. I had been wanting to see that movie and was glad to have something to do for the evening.

I had met Sarah just a couple of years earlier when she hired me to redecorate her house. We became fast friends and always had lots of fun together—whatever we were doing. She got my sense of humor, and I could make her laugh. She had a great sense of humor as well.

I always thought I was probably a bad influence on Sarah. When I first started working on her house, if something went wrong she would say, "Oh, sugar." I thought that was so sweet and such a nice southern way to cuss a little bit. After Sarah had been around me for a few years, though, I hate to say it but "sugar" had turned to "shit." And Sarah was saying, "Oh, shit" about as often as I was.

Sarah picked me up and we headed south to the

The Flat Tire

theater. Florence was about forty miles away from Boonetown, and I knew the city pretty well. Florence was the closest city to Boonetown that had some good shopping options and some medical specialists. Plus, it had a university, and that's where I had spent four years in college.

Mom would often take one of us kids to Florence to see the orthodontist or dermatologist. In addition to my extreme height and skinniness, I had a pretty bad case of acne in high school, so I was really cute. This dermatologist treated it with a really painful process that didn't seem to do any good.

After he had assaulted my acne with a scalpel, he would then rub this alcohol mixture all over the fresh open wounds on my face to give it a nice burn — you could actually hear it sizzle. The last step was putting my face in this metal shoe-box with an ultraviolet light to, I assume, bake away any future zits.

When I left there, I looked so handsome. Sort of a war-torn look with lots of red, bleeding splotches on my face. I still am not sure why I continued to go, maybe I was addicted to the pain or, more likely, the Shoney's strawberry pie.

At that time, Florence had a Shoney's and we didn't have one back home. Back then, strawberry pie and hot fudge cake were their big claims to fame. Supposedly, they trucked-in all the huge fresh strawberries directly from California, and we thought that was really cool.

I couldn't wait to have a slice of that fresh strawberry pie after a meal at Shoney's. It seemed like a huge thrill at the time. Now, I find it almost repulsive. I am not sure if they still bring the strawberries in from

California, though, so that may be the problem. Over the years, the strawberries became big, hollow and flavorless.

Boonetown finally did get a Shoney's a few years later, while I was in college I think, and we ate there often. My family went there for the breakfast bar after church most Sundays. Unfortunately, the management was lax and the place began to fall apart. After many years of neglect, holes in the carpet were so big that you could see the concrete sub-floor. My decision to quit going to Shoney's came the night I was eating there, at a booth, and a big piece of heavy vinyl wallpaper literally fell off the wall and landed on my table.

Florence really gained my esteem when they got a new mall. I was really excited. It was the first mall that I had any real access to, and it had some nice department stores. At the same time Florence also got a new, multi-screen movie theater. Boonetown only had one theater and never got current films. I think *Smokey and the Bandit* played at the local theater for about four months one year. We all know it was a classic, but everyone in town had seen it about six times. So when I was in high school, my friend and I would go down to the mall to hang out, shop, and then maybe go see a movie. I would also end up seeing many films in that theater during my college years in Florence.

The University of North Alabama is in the older, downtown part of Florence and was my college home from 1980 till 1984. I lived in Rivers Hall, a really ugly modern dormitory on a hilly campus with a lot of other (more-attractive) historic buildings. Unfortunately, the dorms were all built in the 1960's

The Flat Tire

and were very basic brick boxes.

I had really dreaded moving into a dorm. To make matters worse, I had decided to attend UNA at the last minute, after any potential roommates had already found roommates. So I had no choice but to take an assigned roommate and hope for the best. This did not go well—at all. I repeat: "Did not go well."

His name was Bart Bork. Bart Bork from Pittsburg, Pennsylvania. This was my new roommate.

I met him the day we were moving in together. His parents had driven him down from Pittsburg and were with him when we met. I thought this was so very odd that he had come so far away from his home. He explained to me later that he had heard that UNA had a really good baseball program, and he was going to be a walk-on and make the team.

Now, as you may know by this point, fashion and shoes are of great interest to me. Sports are not. It was obvious to me from the moment my roommate and I met that we had nothing in common. Bart told me that, on the day he and his parents got to town, they took him to the local Kmart and bought him supplies for his dorm room and three pairs of shoes. I, of course, thought he probably bought a pair of tennis shoes, a pair of Docksides, and a pair of Bass loafers. These were the three pairs of shoes virtually every male came to college with that year, all across the country, so I was not out of line in thinking this.

I was wrong.

They bought him three pairs of *identical* white tennis shoes. I think they were Puma brand, but I can't be sure. Again, I thought it was odd, but thought maybe he was going to wear one pair to play sports, one pair to his classes, and maybe save the other pair for nice occasions.

I was wrong again.

He threw all three pairs of shoes under his bed and every morning would fish out a left and a right shoe. They were no longer pairs of shoes, just six individual shoes. He would randomly choose a left and a right shoe every time he dressed. This drove me nuts, but he thought it was completely normal.

A couple of days later, he left—in two of his Puma tennis shoes—to go *walk-on* to the baseball team. He walked back to the dorm later that day, still not a member of the team. This was no surprise to me. I just had a feeling. He loved to talk big and to brag. It was quickly apparent to me that he was full of shit, and I also had a feeling he wouldn't be at UNA very long.

He was, however, at UNA long enough to make my life miserable.

I had made another big mistake when signing up for a dorm room. There was a box on the application that said, "Check here if you want to live on a quiet floor." For some reason, I thought that would be really boring and everyone would be studying all the time and it would be *too quiet*. I felt like it would be a whole floor of science club members. So I did not check the box.

I cannot tell you how badly I screwed that up.

I, unfortunately, had a lot of early-morning classes. This was back when you went to college and you actually *went to* classes in *actual* classrooms. Unlike now, when you *go* to college but end up taking most of your classes online. So, I needed sleep. I had to be up early and walk to class. I guess I was a radical type and thought you needed to actually attend classes. He didn't see it that way and took more of an only-when-in-the-mood approach to attending his classes. He was up most of the night.

Most everyone on my floor was doing some sort of drugs. There was definitely a party atmosphere, and most of the guys blasted their stereos at full volume until the early morning hours. They certainly weren't spending any time going to classes. At least my roommate didn't do drugs. Bart Bork was just a nut.

After he failed to make the baseball team, he joined the ROTC and became a Ranger. Ranger Bart—as I called him from then on—became obsessed with his Ranger duties. At least this stopped some of the sports talk, but I was no more interested in his Ranger duties than sports.

Ranger Bart would also tell me about all the pretty girls he was dating (I never saw one), and all the weekend camping trips he was taking, and how he excelled on the Ranger training course.

After a weekend of training in rappelling, he excitedly told me about how great he was at rappelling down the sides of both buildings and mountains. The training course I had seen on campus housed a twenty-foot-high wall that the Rangers practiced on, but Ranger Bart made it sound more like he had been walking down the side of a glass skyscraper.

Late one night, when I was already in bed trying to get to sleep, he told me he was going to rappel down the side of our dormitory building. He felt he was more than up to the task. We were on the fifth floor. We also were in a set of metal bunk beds. I then kind of dozed off, thinking he was just talking. I awoke to some tugging on the bed. He had tied rope to the bed frame and thrown the rope out the window. He was preparing to go out on the window ledge. I knew that the little bit of rope he had shown me wouldn't make it even half-way down, and I also knew that he would kill himself.

It was a very challenging moral dilemma. I was suddenly having visions of entire nights of uninterrupted sleep and a quiet room all to myself without having to listen to all of his bullshit stories. I even briefly thought that no one would know if I sort of helped things along and untied the rope. But I felt morally compelled to at least *try* to talk him out of his inevitable plunge to sudden death.

After some discussion, he decided to wait until the next day to rappel down the side of the building. I felt this was a good solution. I could then be far away—innocently in class—if he plunged to his death. I had even practiced acting surprised when I got the news.

He never did rappel out the window. Just like I said, Ranger Bart was all talk.

Once, he bought food and was going to learn to cook in our dorm room...in an electric popcorn maker. He only made a huge mess, which he never cleaned up, and then shoved the mess under his bed with his six identical shoes. He then bought an electric guitar and an amp, and was determined to become a great musician *that night*. The next week it was squirrel hunting.

The one thing good about Ranger Bart was that his attention span was short, so he didn't indulge in any of his new hobbies for more than a couple of days.

The Flat Tire

But, each time, those two days were long ones for me. That one semester with Ranger Bart seemed about two years long.

Fortunately, I met a nice guy in my algebra class who also wanted to switch roommates at the end of the semester. We made arrangements to move in together after Christmas, and I thought that time would never arrive. But it did. After I changed roommates, I actually began to enjoy living in the dorm.

Although, when I look back on it now, I realize the dorm itself was pretty much a dump. We had no cable TV, no phones in the rooms, some junky furniture and a Ping-Pong table in the community lounge, and, most annoyingly, elevators that never worked. In addition to that, we always seemed to be having false fire alarms and would have to evacuate the building in the middle of the night. This became a huge issue when I moved in with my new roomie on the eighth floor—that's a lot of steps at three a.m.

I certainly couldn't have imagined, when I started at UNA, that college would end up being the setting for my greatest accomplishment in sport. Actually, I was pretty sure I would never have any accomplishments in sport, but there was this one.

I never played any organized sports in grade school, high school, or college. I never really enjoyed team sports and wasn't good at them. But during my first semester at UNA, I took tennis for my physical education requirement and was surprised that I was fairly decent at it. On a tennis court, I had good ground strokes and could cover the net well. But once my opponent figured out that I was really slow moving around the court, he could easily beat me.

The Flat Tire

I was also pretty good at Ping-Pong. I had been able to beat all of the guys in my high school gym class and almost all the guys in the dorm. Except this *one* guy who was scary-quick and really good.

So this brought on another moral dilemma. One night, the scary-quick Ping-Pong guy got dumped by his girlfriend, got drunk, and tried to jump out our eighth-floor window. He was a good friend of my roommate (the new one, not Ranger Bart), and had come over to drown his sorrows in our room. My roommate would calm him down, and then a few minutes later he would be back at the window, talking about jumping.

It did briefly cross my mind that, if he jumped, I could be the Ping-Pong champ of the dorm. What an intoxicating idea it was, but I thought better of it.

After two semesters of tennis, for my next P.E. requirement, I chose badminton. I figured racket sports were my forte. And I really liked it. I was good at it too. The badminton court was much smaller than a tennis court so my slow movement was not nearly as much of a problem. My long arms and height were a huge asset. Even in college, I continued to get teased about my height and skinniness a lot — not nearly as much as high school, but still plenty. At least now it was very useful. We just practiced and learned the rules the first few weeks and then had a tournament toward the end of the semester.

I couldn't help but notice a couple of the UNA football players were in my class. They stuck together, and, since they were part of a winning football program, they had a healthy bit of attitude. You could tell by their body language they expected to be the number one team.

I asked a guy that I had been practicing with to be my partner for the tournament. I was a sophomore. He was an equally skinny but much shorter freshman. Surprisingly, we made our way through the first few matches of the tournament, winning fairly easily. I was completely shocked by this since I was usually the one left standing when my classmates chose-up teams. (The only time anyone ever wanted to pick me for their team was on Red-and-Blue day in grade school. It was because I was the best sign-maker in school, and they knew our team would have great banners. They regretted their decision soon enough, though, when we played a game.)

The football players were also winning the early games in their bracket.

All of a sudden(it seemed), it was announced that we would be playing the football-boys in the finals. It was only a college-badminton-class tournament, but suddenly it took on great importance. It seemed like this could be some sort of vindication for all the years of my feeling inferior to the athletically gifted boys in high school and college. UNA had a very successful Division II football team, and these were some of the top seniors, so you can imagine how much pressure they felt to beat these two skinny underclassmen.

I don't think I've ever concentrated as much, or played as hard, as I did in that match. I played well, and my partner did too. We were focused. I could tell that the football players were surprised that we were actually close to beating them, and they began to really get nervous. They had come into the match with way too much confidence. And they left the match in shock.

We ended up winning the match that day. It was close, but the skinny-boys prevailed, and I left feeling rather euphoric. I really thought that some of our classmates should have at least carried us around the gym on their shoulders, but none of them saw any need to do so.

I wish I could remember the name of my partner from that class. He was such a nice guy. I'd love to play a little badminton with him again, and talk about the day we beat two football stars.

I don't know why I thought about that as we were walking through the parking lot in Florence after seeing a movie that Christmas night, but I did. The movie was quite good, but also long, so it was around midnight when we returned to the car.

I said, "Um, Sarah? You have a flat tire."

Sarah, immediately said, "No, I don't," fully confident she was right.

Now, I am the first to admit that I am not very mechanical and don't know a lot about cars, but I am fully capable of spotting a flat tire. And this was not a tire just low on air, this tire was completely flat. The rim was literally touching the ground.

"Sarah, it's definitely flat," I said.

"No, it's not," she said from the other side of the car.

"Well, come around here and explain what this is."

By this time, she realized I was serious and came around to look. I said, "Sarah, do you have a spare tire?"

"Yes, I do."

"Great" I said, "where is it?"

"It's right there" she said, as she pointed to the flat tire.

"Oh, shit." I replied.

Sarah was not big on auto maintenance—at all. So I was very surprised when she said, "It's not a problem. I have a can of Fix-a-Flat in my trunk."

I was skeptical. Not skeptical that she actually had a can of Fix-a-Flat, but skeptical that a can of Fix-a-Flat could fix this tire. It was flat. Completely flat. Sarah was undeterred by my concerns.

Sarah had a way of doing that—moving straight ahead no matter what anyone was saying. I liked that about her. Under the nearby parking-lot light, we tried to read the instructions. This was before either of us had cell phones, so it wasn't as easy to call someone for help. And it was late, too, so we didn't want to wake anyone up. The Fix-a-Flat definitely seemed to be the best option.

The other theaters were emptying out while we were contemplating the situation. A lot of *normal* people might have been distressed by this, but not us, we thought it was funny. For some reason we thought it was *really* funny. Laugh-out-loud funny. Especially when we read the instructions on the can and they repeatedly warned us that using this product incorrectly could cause the tire to explode.

I was trying to do what my mom would have expected of me, and so I sacrificed myself to be the one to put the spray into the tire. I thought *I might as well bear the brunt of the explosion since Sarah drove us to the theater.*

If you have never used this product, it looks like a can of spray paint with a little hose, about a quarter-inch in diameter by six inches long, attached to the spray nozzle. You put the little hose onto the tire valve and then press the button on the can to start the flow of the "stuff" into the tire. You are supposed to hold the hose tightly onto the valve.

But the valve and the hose stem weren't a perfect fit. It kept sliding off. Every time it would slide off the tire valve, the spray contents would go all over my fingers and hand. It seemed like I could only get a few seconds of spray into the tire before it would slip off again and the spray would cover my fingers.

It didn't take long to realize that what I was spraying into the tire was some type of strong, sticky glue. Within minutes, my fingers became stuck together. This was very strong glue to say the least. I suddenly had two mittens for hands and no use of individual fingers. I felt like my hands had been dipped into a vat of superglue. I was convinced this *stuff*, *wha*tever it was, was not helping the tire, because the tire was not inflating.

We were still quite amused by all of this. When I held up my two mittens and showed them to Sarah, she really lost it. We both lost it. We were laughing hard, and the people in the parking lot had begun to stare. They also made a wide path around our car as they walked to their car. Not one of them offered any help. I think they thought we were drunk or high, and that was a safe assumption since we were both pretty much acting that way.

Sarah began reading the directions again, trying to figure out what we were doing wrong. The tire was still completely flat and I felt like I had just about emptied the can. I kept telling Sarah that it was not working. She remained calm and kept reading the instructions. Then she discovered the problem.

According to the fine print, the tired would not begin to inflate until we started driving.

"No way," I said.

"I swear that's what it says," Sarah replied.

We both looked at the deflated tired and looked at each other and burst out laughing again.

Then we both said, "No way!" at the same time.

She went on reading, "Be careful not to overfill the tire, or it can explode when you begin driving."

We laughed even louder.

"Well, at least we will be in the car when the tire blows off," I said.

More laughing. We decided to give it a try.

"Uh, Sarah," I said, "we have another problem. This little hose is glued to the tire valve. It will *not* come off."

She, thinking I was joking again, reached down to pull it off and quickly discovered it was glued to that valve stem—tight—just as I had said. Again, we looked at each other and laughed even louder. I was afraid to pull it too hard and tear off the valve stem. Then there would absolutely be no way to fix it.

By this time the parking lot was just about empty and we were still standing there, laughing. The tire, the can stuck to it, my fingers glued together—I don't think I've ever laughed so hard in my life. It just all seemed so funny.

After our laughter again died down, I told Sarah to start driving around the parking lot and I would watch—from a good distance—and see if the tire

The Flat Tire

inflated, or the tire exploded, or the can exploded, or who knows what.

I stood watching as the car started moving around the parking lot and every time Sarah passed under a light, it appeared that the tire was getting bigger. It was hard to tell, of course, considering the can was clanking and bouncing up and down off the pavement. Shockingly, the can didn't explode, nor did the tire.

Eventually after a few laps the can fell off, and the only thing remaining stuck to the valve stem was the little six inch hose. I flagged Sarah down and got in the car after the tire appeared to be about fifty-percent full. We could *not* believe that this was working.

There was a Hardee's across the highway that appeared to still be open, and I asked Sarah to drive me over there so I could try to get some of the glue off my hands. I wouldn't let her stop driving though. I asked her to keep circling the parking lot to inflate the tire while I was in the rest room. When I was finally able to separate my fingers and got back to the car, I was simply amazed that the tire looked almost fully inflated. When I got in the car and gave the news to Sarah, we broke into uncontrollable laughter—again.

We decided to get on the road home immediately, since we had no idea if the tire would stay inflated, or might continue to inflate until it exploded. All during the ride home we laughed. When we arrived, we were shocked that we had made it, with a now-fully-inflated tire.

I was still hoarse from all the laughing when I returned to work a couple of days later. One of my employees stopped by my office and said they saw me at the movies. I sort of panicked at the thought. I immediately said, "Did you see us in the theater, or in the parking lot?"

Thankfully, he said he had seen me inside the theater. I was fully prepared to deny being in the parking lot. I can't imagine what he would have thought if he had seen us acting completely crazy, laughing our heads off, trying to fix a flat.

ALL IN THE BIG-HEADED FAMILY

We have always been called "big-headed", the Evers family men. It's not about ego, though, or that we think we are really cool. It's about actual head size.

I am a big person, six-foot-six tall. My head size seems to be proportionate. I have to order all my hats online in a double-extra-large size.

My brother, Mike, and his sons are referred to as "the big-headed Evers" out at the K.C. Club where they often hang out. That's the Knights of Columbus Club, a place for Catholic men to gather. My nephews are members too, and they also have to order their hats in extra-large sizes. They aren't nearly as tall as I am, so I think they get a little more teasing about head size than I do, but they have always taken it well. What choice do they have really?

I wouldn't say I am proud of big-headedness or ashamed of it either. I don't think about it a lot. It's just a fact of life: big heads run in my family.

They call the Evers men from Palmetto (a neighboring town) "the little-headed Evers." They hang out at the K.C. Club as well. They are smaller-framed people and their heads don't look weird or anything. They are proportionate too. But I think they also get their fair share of taunting. If you hang out at the K. C. Club, taunting is pretty much a given.

The subject of big heads would often come up at work. Salesmen would stop by our business and give us baseball caps with their logos, but I never could wear them. They would be so tight that, even with the gusset let all the way out, I would have a deep red indention around my head after wearing one. The same was true for my brother.

I grew up in the family business. My father started it when he got out of the Air Force in 1955. The business was always there, like another member of the family, discussed during dinner and taken into consideration before every family vacation or school event. Could Dad get away? What was going on at work? And, just like a sick relative, the business always needed attention.

I started out sweeping floors, emptying garbage, and helping in the office after school and during the summers. My brother, four years older than I am, was already working as a helper in the HVAC department and running equipment on construction sites.

We seldom saw each other since he went straight to the job sites and I went straight to the office. That was probably a good thing since we were both still recovering from sharing a room in our younger years and from the deep-seated hatred for each other produced by that cohabitation.

The family business even influenced my course of study. I had backed out of going to architecture school (my first inclination) and chose a business major. My double-major in marketing and computer information systems, for some crazy reason, seemed like a good decision at the time.

I came to absolutely loathe the computer information course-of-study. I was learning to write programs in COBOL and Fortran and other languages that turned out to be just as valuable as the Latin class I had in high school. Latin was a dead language and I never really understood why they were teaching that in high school rather than a language you might actually use. By the time I got my business degree, and personal computers were introduced, all the computer languages I had learned in college were pretty much on their death bed too.

That was really ok by me. I had already determined that if I had to write computer programs and design systems for a living, I might as well shoot myself — right in my big, enormous head.

My dad had convinced me to work in the family construction business. I had been coming home on the weekends, doing payroll and bookkeeping, and it seemed like the right thing to do. He had already had his first heart attack during my junior year of college — I felt like he needed me.

My brother was now working full-time in the business as well, so the three Evers men in my family were now also three Evers men in the family business. I was the youngest.

One of the first things I did after I graduated from college was to put our company on a new computer system. My dad was reluctant about the "computerization" of the company, but when he saw all the job-cost reports we could now generate, his attitude began to change.

He would still tell all his friends, "Computers in the

front office are just fine, but there will never be a computer in *my* office." And there wasn't one in his office until years later when he found out he could get stock market reports and constant stock updates.

Then he changed his mind.

I hooked one up.

I found a site that allowed him to input his stock portfolio, and then he could monitor his stock values at any moment.

He loved it.

After he had been using this system a couple of years, he came into my office and told me that all his friends were talking about this new thing called "the internet." He wanted to know how he could get on it.

I said, "Dad, you know that stock program you check about ten times a day?"

"Yeah." he said.

I said, "Well, it is coming to you via the internet. You are on the internet every day."

He left the room both shocked and delighted.

Later that day I heard him on the phone talking to one of his buddies. "Man, I've been busy on the internet today. Yeah, just checking my stocks. You ever use it? You should get hooked up."

One thing that I was always proud of is that my dad was the first small-business owner in Boonetown to offer a group health insurance plan. This was so long ago that Blue Cross actually gave him a check book from their bank, and he would write checks from *their* account to pay the claims. Can you imagine?

This is one thing that my dad, my brother and I have always agreed on. Health insurance should not just be for the privileged few. My dad always offered health insurance and paid a large chunk of the cost—long before there were any mandates to do so. Our employees always appreciated it. I did too, and still do.

As I get older, I find more and more reasons to go to the doctor and to use my health insurance. It's nothing I enjoy. I still go though, because I want to try to live as healthy a life as possible, for as long as possible.

Recently, my doctor suggested I try the new genetic testing for cancer. It's a risk assessment, and, considering my family history, I thought it was probably a good idea. My doctor knew that my mother had died of ovarian cancer, so once I told him that my brother was taking treatments for prostate cancer, he thought it was time. I had also recently had a couple of cousins diagnosed with other types of cancer. I'd been hearing about these new tests, but didn't really know that much about them.

Dr. Harmon said that it was a very simple procedure involving bloodwork and a follow-up phone call to discuss the results. So I said, "Sure, sign me up."

Actually, there was a lot more to it than he said.

First of all, I went and had the blood drawn. But then I got a call from the insurance company. Before they would process the bloodwork, they would need to do a counseling session by phone to make sure I understood the gravity of the information I might receive. This seemed a bit concerning to me, but I was too far into it to turn back now.

The counseling session was set up during *another* call, where they advised me to reserve at least an hour for the counseling phone call. An hour? What the hell were we going to talk about for an hour?

As it turns out, we had plenty to talk about. The call, according to the advisor, would be a deep dive into my health and cancer history, as well as that of my family. The specialized nurse that called was extremely nice, and I could hear her doing lots and lots of typing on her end of the call as I spoke with her.

We went over my mother's cancer diagnosis and all the details I could remember about the progression of her illness, the age she got it, and any other cancer history in her family (there was none that I knew of). I told them about my brother and his cancer, and about my dad's mother who I felt died of *some* type of cancer. I just remember her having a tumor and having to have a hand removed before she died a few years later. Then I mentioned some cousins of mine who had cancer.

She continued to type. Then there was a long pause.

I was wondering what she was thinking.

Then she said, "Hold on, I want to look something up." This concerned me a bit.

She continued to read and then asked a couple more questions.

She said there was a cancer syndrome (or something like that) that could cause the various types of cancer that I had reported in my family members. I thought this was rather strange, since the types of cancer in my family members were all very different.

She went on to explain that this gene, or something like that, might be something they would want to check for in my bloodwork. (Forgive my incorrect terminology, but I was really not expecting to get into all of this in the conversation, and I was quite unprepared and didn't take notes.)

I had assumed that they would just look for all types of cancer in the bloodwork, but after talking with her, it seemed they based some of the testing on my family history. She was beginning to concern me as she continued to question me about this "cancer syndrome."

Then suddenly she let out a big sigh of relief.

"Oh good," she said, "this doesn't apply to you after all. We don't need to worry about that."

"Why do you say that?" I asked, still concerned.

I swear to God what I am about to tell you is the truth and is exactly how the rest of the conversation went.

She continued, "You don't have to worry about this because, in further reading, I see that this cancer syndrome only occurs in people with extremely large heads."

"What?" I said. "What size heads?"

She replied, "Well, it says here people with 'extremely large heads', so I don't think you need to worry."

"Wait a minute." I said. "What are we talking about here, size-wise? What do you mean by *extremely* large? Are we talking *volleyball-size, basketball-size*, or *beachball-size* heads?"

"I'm not sure," she said.

"You don't understand," I said, "my family members have been called the 'big-headed Evers' for years, and I order all my hats in double-extra-large! I need to know what size you mean. Are we talking just *extra-*

large heads or *circus-freak*-sized?"

I think she thought I was trying to be funny, but I could never get her to give me any size comparison.

It continued to run through my big head until weeks later, when I finally got the call to go over my test results. She said that I didn't show any genetic markers to be concerned about and that everything with the genetic testing looked good. I was thankful that I didn't have to worry about the large-headed-cancer syndrome.

But then she went on to say that the genetic factors only accounted for a very small percentage of the various causes of cancer, so I should continue to do all the other usual cancer screenings and tests that were available.

In other words, I had gone through this exercise and basically been told to keep doing what I was doing.

Except now I was more conscious than ever of my freak-sized head.

Once I found out that we were cleared of the large-headed cancer syndrome, I could not wait to tell my brother and my nephews. They in turn told the group at the K. C. Club, which caused roars of laughter from the small-headed Evers and the other average-headed club members.

I truly wish I had gone to share the story myself. I would have loved to have heard the laughs. I didn't really think my nephews would even tell the other members—fearing years and years of big-head jokes. As it turned out, they could not hold such a good story back and told it anyway. That's one thing all the Evers men—no matter how different—had in common. We all love to laugh.

My dad had passed away in 2006, long before all these big-headed cancer revelations. He had a massive heart attack and died after a two-month struggle. My brother and I were left the family business in an equal partnership. My brother's oldest son was already working for the company when my dad died, and my brother's younger son joined the company after he got out of college.

It was great to have the young blood in the company. Thankfully, both of my nephews have remained in the business. That was a big relief to me and my brother.

My brother Mike and I were completely different in many ways and had little in common. Over the years, though, we found that we agreed on most everything involving the business and many things outside of the business, like politics.

At one point we even discovered that our musical tastes did intersect at the crossroads of Bruce Springsteen. Mike was a rabid fan of his, while I was more of an average fan I suppose. But there was one moment in time where me, my brother, and my sister Janice were all at the same Springsteen concert.

By the time my dad died, Mike and I had both been in the family business, in one capacity or another, for close to thirty years.

Mike and I always tried to keep things light and would often try to one-up each other with funny employee stories. He definitely had the advantage since he was around the large crews in the field and all of the sub-contractors, while I was mostly in the office with the small group of the same employees each day.

One day, he couldn't wait to tell me what had

happened on an out-of-town job he had just returned from.

They were finishing up a project at a large plant in a town a few hours away, so the crews were staying in a hotel. After work had ended that day, everyone had gone back to the hotel, cleaned up, and headed over to the Shoney's seafood bar for dinner.

Mike said that the supervisor, Johnny, who was known for being very loud, was ribbing a worker named Danny all the way to Shoney's about his big-floral-print Hawaiian shirt. Danny was the last guy I would have expected to see in a big-floral-print shirt, (he was kind of a short and stocky guy) and I can't imagine that it would have been flattering on him, but I also can't imagine that Danny would care in the least what anyone thought about his wardrobe choices.

Mike had finished loading his plate at the salad bar and was back at the table. Johnny (the loud one) was still at the bar loading his plate when a floral-print-sleeved arm reached over on the bar and got all the remaining shrimp.

This really pissed Johnny off, so he said loudly as he passed his friend, "Why don't you leave something for the rest of us, you fat son-of-a-bitch," and then headed back to the table.

But when he looked at the table, he could see Danny already sitting there in his big-floral-print Hawaiian shirt.

Johnny looked back to see a large woman in a big-floral-print muumuu scraping shrimp off of her plate back onto the seafood bar.

He figured the damage had been done and settled in to eat, but I bet that poor woman still has flashbacks every time she goes to a salad bar.

Not to be outdone, I told Mike about the lunch I had with Betty out at the Copper Lamp Restaurant.

Betty worked for me in the office for years and was absolutely hilarious. She had a sharp, quick wit, and we had great fun together. Her hobby was sewing clothes for young children and infants, and she was very talented.

During lunch, Betty was showing me photos of all the beautiful work she had been doing. Hand-smocked pink dresses for little girls and long, highly-detailed, lace-covered christening gowns for infants. These were the epitome of innocence and purity. Betty took great pride in her intricate and detailed sewing, and loved to talk about it.

Our waitress began to take great interest in the photos and was asking Betty a lot of questions. She wanted to know if Betty did custom sewing for the public and Betty told her she did, assuming the waitress had a small child she might want a dress for.

Betty began to ask her what kind of sewing she needed but the waitress was a bit evasive. The waitress then asked Betty if she ever made outfits with Velcro closures and if she ever made any adult clothing. Betty said, "Not often, but I have."

The waitress kept asking strange questions about these outfits, like how washable they were and if she ever used snap-tape for quick removal.

I knew something was up, but still wasn't sure where she was going, until she finally let the cat out of the bag. She said she was a stripper over at the Boobie Bungalow Club in Montery and needed a baby-doll outfit for her act.

She went on to say that it had to be made with Velcro closures and snaps so it would break-away easily. She also said it needed to be very durable since it got thrown on the floor and stepped on a lot.

Now, keep in mind that by this time, I was about to wet my pants. I wanted to laugh so hard I couldn't stand it. Betty was quite shocked. Betty, with her razor-sharp wit, was—for the first time I had ever witnessed—at a complete loss for words. Lunch never tasted so good.

Even Mike had to admit that I had the best story in the office that day.

When my brother died, suddenly, of a massive heart attack in 2021, much like my dad had fifteen-years earlier, it once again made me realize how short life can be and that I needed to take advantage of every moment.

I am just sixty—I hear it's the new forty—but I will admit I have spent some time thinking about my odds of having the same outcome. It isn't a happy thought, but it isn't unrealistic either.

The good thing is that my brother's two sons are now my partners in the business. It suddenly hit me though, that we are once again a trio of Evers men in the ownership.

But now, I am the oldest and they are the youngest. I liked it a lot better when I was the youngest—not all that many years ago—but I was not consulted on this change.

So here I am, the elder Evers.

I am still trying to remain relevant, but that is hard too. I'm easily distracted. It is obvious my younger counterparts are doing a far better job running the company than I ever did, so at least I don't worry about that.

Even if I am now the *oldest* owner of the family business, I am not the sole owner. I have the next generation.

I guess that's what a family business is all about. Passing things on to the younger ones, the ones with great big heads full of new ideas.

THE GRAND SCHEME OF THINGS

They aren't as young as they used to be, The Harlettes. I heard Bette Midler referring to her back-up singers as Harlettes, so I started calling my helpers The Harlettes as well. It stuck. And they have stuck. They have stuck with me through thick and thin.

My Harlettes are the ones that will spend hours breaking-down boxes and bagging-up the mountains of trash you have accumulated from unpacking a tractor-trailer-load of furniture and accessories. They will and they have. Lucky for me they are great friends too.

One of the Harlettes even had to overcome severe claustrophobia. It happened when I was working on a penthouse for one of the Atlanta Braves. She rode an elevator up thirty-two floors to help me on that job. She survived. And after about four days of that, I think she was over her claustrophobia—another added benefit of being my friend.

Incidentally, that was the second home I decorated for that baseball player. When he got traded to the Braves, I had to get his new Atlanta penthouse ready in a big hurry. He wanted it finished by the time he got finished with spring training.

They figured out fairly quickly that I wasn't much of a

baseball fan because I kept asking, "Now when exactly will he be home from *spring break*?" For some reason, I just couldn't get "spring training" to stick in my head. Regardless of my lack of baseball knowledge, I did get the place done on-time, and it was pretty fabulous, I must say.

People see us—me and The Harlettes—on my project set-up days and think we are having so much fun. We are. We laugh and cut-up the whole time. We are also working our asses off the whole time. It seems people don't notice the work as much as they do the fun we are having, though. Often they ask if I am looking for any new Harlettes. This one delivery guy said that his mother really wanted to join our group, and he said that she had lots of great decorating ideas. "Hold it right there," I said. "She is disqualified."

See, one of the main rules for helping me is *not* to have any ideas.

All of my helpers have great taste, and I will occasionally ask them for an opinion. But, honestly, the main thing I am looking for is a lot of ooh-ing and aah-ing over the work I am doing. Yeah, I know that sounds like I am an arrogant ass, but it's my process and it has worked for this long, so why change?

Unfortunately, as time is flying by, I can't help notice that we have slowed down a bit. Far be it from me to be indelicate, but all my helpers are now in their seventies. Since they have always acted and looked so young, I haven't thought about our ages very much. Lately though, it's obvious that none of us can put out the work like we used to.

We need more breaks and longer ones at that. That's all ok, because lately my jobs aren't that stressful or on tight deadlines, so we don't have to be as fast as in the past. Still, it's one more of those little reminders that time is moving swiftly.

I went with two of The Harlettes to a wedding last weekend. It was a really nice ceremony. The vows were out in a botanical garden. There was a string quartet playing when we walked down the path to our seats, and they played throughout the service. I even commented to one of my friends that I had never seen a bride walk down the aisle to *La Vie en Rose* before. It was really lovely.

After the ceremony, as we were walking out, Maggie said, "That was really pretty, but I thought it would have been nice if they had had some music."

Sarah said, "I thought the same thing."

I said, "Where were you two? They played all through the service."

"Well, I never heard it," they both said.

I said, "What did you think I was talking about when I mentioned *La Vie en Rose*?"

Maggie said, "I thought you were talking about all the roses they had placed down the aisle."

We've had a great laugh about it. We laugh at ourselves a lot.

My design work started out as a sideline gig that I did on the weekends, but turned into a career that involved hundreds of projects — large and small. One of the best things about the work is that, even though the actual design work happens mostly in my head when I am alone or driving or walking, the execution of those jobs often happens with friends. It's a fun way to work. Most of the memories of these jobs are inextricably tied to the friends that have helped me so much along the way and to so many of the clients who have become long-time friends.

I never studied interior design, drawing, or architecture or any of that. Sometimes I wish I had, and then at other times I'm glad I didn't. My work is very organic. Ideas just come to me. There are no formulas and no guidelines I use. I just come up with a concept, lock it into my brain, and try to make it happen.

It's hard for me to talk about design without reflecting on the bigger lessons I have learned. I always thought that as I aged, I might be able to turn off my creative mind and relax more, maybe just read a book, or sit in a chair and watch the sunset. I really envy people that can flip that switch and just go to the beach.

I can't.

Unfortunately, or maybe fortunately, getting older has only seemed to create more of a sense of urgency in my projects. I feel that I have no time to waste, so I must be even more productive.

It's that creative guilt I feel. It gnaws at me. It makes me yearn to be doing something that will lead to some kind of a finished result — something that adds beauty, or enhances life. It's a constant need to be producing something or at least be thinking about a new project. Some of you will probably think I am nuts. Many of you will know exactly what I mean.

I had these feelings as long as I can remember — since I was twelve or thirteen. I didn't grow up in a world that embraced creatives, or nurtured them, so it took me a long time to just accept it and find a support system of other creative people. I do wish I could turn it off at times—all those creative juices—but I can never seem to completely shut it down. I've even gotten burned-out on design at times—after taking on too many jobs—and slowed down or stopped for a while. But that usually didn't last very long. Those creative urges are back soon enough.

Here is one piece of advice that I will share. If you aren't the creative type and you want to hire a designer, do some homework. Find one you can trust, not just one who is available. When there is mutual trust between the client and the designer, that's when the magic happens. If you don't really know your designer and aren't sure if you like their work, you should not hire them. It is an exercise in frustration for everyone involved.

All of my favorite projects are the ones with clients that trusted me and believed in me. I always left those jobs proud of my work, and I think the client was proud too. So many creatives aren't necessarily working for the money, we are working for the love of the craft. I know that has always been true for me. We really value those clients that let us push the limits of our creativity.

Once upon a time, I was asked to work for an executive that everyone hated. He had moved to Tennessee with a large company and wanted a progressive, modern design in the corporate offices. This man had been working in major cities. He had been exposed to a lot of good design.

At first, I was intimidated. His reputation fell somewhere between ogre and tyrant, but he kept having his managers ask me to do more work, so I figured he must like what I was doing. They told me that he wanted design that looked like New York—not Boonetown. I loved his way of thinking because that was exactly the kind of work I wanted to do.

After just a couple of smaller projects, he assigned me some very large design jobs at their corporate headquarters. I still could only assume he liked my work, since I never dealt directly with him.

Finally, one day, as I was completing one of the large jobs for him, he took me aside—we had not ever had a private conversation until this day—and told me that he loved my work and was really pleased with what I had done.

This was a no-nonsense guy who did not casually throw around compliments, so I knew he meant it. He even had me do work at his home and continued to hire me after he moved to another company in another city. We became and have remained friends.

Even though some of my clients don't give out a lot of compliments, they have hired me again and again over many years. To me, that is the greatest compliment of all. When someone believes in you, and believes in your talent, it means everything.

TRAVEL PLANS

Some flights are uneventful. Some are downright boring. This one was neither.

I had just taken my seat when a lady cornered the flight attendant, blocked everyone from entry, and began to explain her situation.

"I need to ask a favor," she says.

The flight attendant says, "Ok."

"Could you ask everyone on board the plane to be really quiet when closing the overhead bins? I have hearing damage and that sound really bothers me and I forgot to bring my hearing protection. It is really important because that noise, well, any loud noise, really bothers me. Could you ask them please?"

I tuned-in immediately. This flight attendant looked like a take-no-prisoners gal straight from the Bronx, and I could not wait to hear this answer. But she was very polite and assured the lady she would do everything she could. She even went and found her some disposable earplugs.

The lady profusely thanked the flight attendant — while still blocking all passengers — and again said, "If I had brought my hearing protection, I wouldn't have to ask, but it's really important because, you see, I have this hearing damage."

The flight attendant sort of forcefully guided the lady into her seat while assuring her, again, that she would do everything she could.

I was dying to see how this would play out. As luck would have it, she was sitting right across the aisle from me. She was a sixty-ish, grandmotherly-type lady, ordinary looking, but I could tell she had packed her suitcase full of drama.

As soon as she took her seat, she put both hands over her ears, not in any normal way, but in a very exaggerated way, with a grimaced, pained look on her face. It was as if she was trying to get the passengers to ask her what was wrong. None of them bit though.

By this time, it was becoming very noticeable that the air conditioning on the plane was not working. I was heading back to Nashville after a few days in New York City and it was very hot there. The flight attendant was rather antsy and said that as soon as we closed the doors they could kick on the air conditioning system. So she was in a hurry to get everyone in their seats. People were fanning themselves and complaining about the heat.

I also couldn't help but notice that there was a large group of teenage boys and some of their teachers boarding the flight. The lady with the hearing problem also noticed this. The main teacher/sponsor sat down in front of her and the boys headed further back in the plane. After most of the passengers had boarded, the lady jumped up—once again blocking the aisle—and asked the teacher if they were coming to Tennessee to work for Habitat for Humanity.

"Why, yes!" he said.

"I thought so," she said. "A few days ago, I was on a flight *to* New York and there was a group of students that had been in Tennessee working for Habitat for Humanity and they were on the way home."

"Yes," he said, "there was a group of our students that came down last week and returned earlier in the week. I am sure that was them."

"That's great, they are just angels, I tell you. Every one of them. Angels. I am Mona Marie Jones from Nashville and I woke up last night thinking about the boy that was sitting next to me on that flight. He told me about your school and this wonderful project and I just have to get a message to him. I think his name was Eric, but I am not sure. I am sure that he was the one that *built the door*. He told me he *built the door* on the habitat house. Can you just find the boy that *built the door*. The boy that *built the door* is the boy I want to get a message to. I think his name was Eric, but just make sure he is the boy that *built the door*. He said he gave the new homeowner the key to the door. He *built the door* and gave them the key. See that's why I need to talk to him. It's the key and the door. The door, you see, is the key to his future. I guarantee you, this is the key to his future."

"I'll ask," the man said. I think he was beginning to realize the predicament he was in.

"You should have no problem finding him, he's the one that *built the door*. I'm Mona Marie Jones from Nashville by the way. He must connect *building the door* to the key and to the heart. I lay awake last night thinking that, for Eric, that key *opening* the door, and then his giving the key to the homeowner, is the key to *his* future. He must connect the key opening the door to openness of the heart. His future literally depends on this, trust me. You must find him. I think his name is Eric, but he's the one that *built the door.*"

"I'll relay the message," he said.

"You must tie this into his learning. Tie it in. You must tie it in" she said. "Connect his hands opening the door he built, to opening minds, to opening hearts. You must tie it in. I'm telling you, he must tie it all in. It's the key to his future. Oh, his dad had a dog. That will help you find him. Now you cannot forget this. This is important."

"I think I can find him," the teacher said again, looking around at me and other passengers, begging for help with his look of distress. I wasn't about to intervene. I was sitting next to her and I didn't want to hear this shit for the rest of the flight.

"You must tell him to go to his hands, talk about his hands. He is applying to colleges now and this is the key to his future. I have worked at a college and interviewed prospective students. He must link his hands, and building the door, and the key, and the homeowner. I tell you it's the key to his future. It will get him in any college. He just has to tell them about giving that key to the homeowner. It's the key to his future."

"I'll be sure to tell him."

"He must go to his hands," she said, holding her fists out for emphasis. "He must tell them what it felt like. It's more than a door. It's a house. I am telling you he's going to kill it with *the heart, and the hands, and the door.* It is the key. The key to his future. He just needs to tell them. In the interviews. He has to. You must tell him. He must connect the hands and the key and the house. Tell him. I have severe hearing loss. Our lives are parallel. I understand him. Tell him."

"Ok," the poor man said, looking totally confused.

Did Eric have hearing damage too? I wondered.

Finally, they were about to close the door and the lady had to sit back down. But before she made her way to her seat, she told him again that those kids working for Habitat were absolute angels. She said that, after that prior flight, she had followed Eric to baggage claim and continued talking to him about their Habitat for Humanity project. I thought then that Eric must have truly been a good kid for listening to her throughout an entire flight, because I have no doubt that she talked the entire flight.

And I would really love to hear the translation of her enthusiastic and inspirational message when it finally made it from the teacher back to Eric. I hope the teacher got it right, since it was indeed the key to Eric's future.

After Mona finally sat back down and put her hands up over her ears again, I wondered if she was getting on everyone else's nerves as much as she was mine. As that thought was roaming through my mind, the man sitting across from the teacher got up and took a jacket out of the overhead bin right over Mona's seat. He had been there the entire time, so he could not have helped but hear the woman and all of her conversation, just as I had. After he got his jacket out, he *slammed* the overhead-bin door shut, *loudly*, not once, but *three* times. Mona screamed a bit, looked visually pained, and made fists with her hands.

My question was answered.

I am not one to laugh at anyone's pain, but that was

damn funny.

By the way, did I mention the couple seated right in front of me? They were making out. I'm talking full-out making-out, as if no one else was on the plane. They missed the whole damn thing. The door, the key, the house, the future, everything. They were busy.

What a flight. And we had not even taken off.

That's the thing about travel. You never know what you are going to get. Flights are a pain at best, even if most are pretty uneventful. There is still the airport to deal with and there's always something to test your nerves. I try hard to just numb myself and ignore any drama.

Obviously, it must be worth the hassle and the drama, because we all keep on planning trips and going places.

Recently, someone asked me if I have a bucket list. I don't. I never really liked the whole idea. To me, it's just another way to justify putting off doing things that are important to you. I think if you really want to do something, you should do it now. It will never mean as much to you ten years later when you have "time."

Another thing I don't like is when people say they are going to take this or that trip "when they retire". I get it. It is hard to manage travel when you are working full-time. But one thing I have learned is that the older I get, the harder it is for me to get excited about long travel adventures, especially those overseas ones that involve long flights.

Trust me, you will never have more energy or more desire to do "big" things than you do right now.

Every day your body is aging and who knows what might be around the corner. This might sound gloomy and doom-y, but it is just an unfortunate fact.

I traveled quite a bit when I was younger and I only wish I had traveled much more. It all seemed so much easier then. The hassles were so much less before the pandemic, before 9-11, and so on. Hassles aside, I think the biggest difference was my attitude. My desire to see new places far outweighed the sore back I would inevitably have from flying eight or ten hours in coach. Now, I literally start hurting when I *board* a plane—just in anticipation of the sore back that awaits me when I deplane.

Oh, I still will do it if there is somewhere I *really* want to go, but it takes a lot more desire and a lot more motivation. There are a lot of places I would like to see if the opportunity arises, but I have not made a list. I just like to let those excursions happen if and when the time feels right. I still have not seen a lot of the United States. Those trips are a little less taxing, so I can imagine doing more of that in the future, for sure.

I also find that as I get older, I tend to prefer the idea of returning to my favorite places rather than visiting new ones. It's just easier to go places you are familiar with and know how to get around. I like to have an idea about where to stay and where to eat. It kind of feels like catching up with an old friend. I like to think of cities that way—like old friends.

I have learned a few things over the years that help minimize the pain of travel. For instance, I scour every airline in order to find a direct flight to wherever I am going. Of course, it isn't always possible, but the worry of making a connection, especially with the very short transfer times they give you, is something I don't want or need. So, if at all possible, I always take a direct flight.

Another thing I have streamlined is packing. I never, ever check a bag. I have decided that if it won't go on the plane with me, I must not need it. This is another thing that started because of my height. If the airline loses my luggage, I am completely screwed. I cannot go in a store and buy clothes. Anywhere. So, I became paranoid about losing my luggage and began to make the utmost of my carry-ons. I have a rollerboard suitcase that will fit in the overhead bin, and a tote that will attach to the handle of the suitcase. The tote will fit under the seat. Neither of them hold a lot, but between the two of them, I can get by for up to ten days.

It always amazes me that I usually have the least luggage of my friends on a trip, yet the most clothes. And my clothes are not wrinkled. I really don't know what they pack. But I have found what is—to me anyway— the secret to packing. Compression. The tighter the better. Clothes that are neatly folded and packed very tightly in the suitcase will not move around during travel and therefore will not become wrinkled.

To further ensure unwrinkled clothes, I flatten them out on my bed and stack all the shirts together and then fold them in one big group. I do the same with the pants. The extra thickness of the items folded together will keep creases from forming in the various items. Just hang them up when you get to the hotel. I can't remember the last time I ironed anything at a hotel.

Another thing that helps is to pick a color theme for your trip. This cuts down on the amount of shoes, jackets, and accessories you will need. For example, wardrobe for a New York trip is always mostly black with some nice jeans thrown in.

I also always taxi or Uber to the airport to avoid dealing with the hassle of circling the parking lot looking for a spot and then waiting on shuttles to and from the terminal. The cost of transportation is usually about the same as parking.

These are small things, but they all help me feel less stressed when I travel.

I have travelled a good bit, but not nearly as much as a lot of my friends. Some of them would not even consider me very well-traveled. Then I think about my grandparents, on both sides, and remember that they most likely never even left the state of Tennessee —at least not more than a few times—in their entire lives. They would not believe some of the places I have been. I guess it's all in how you look at it.

Whatever the case, I have never regretted a trip. Travel opens your mind to the world. It often allows you to see your own life in a new light, or from another perspective. Many times, it has helped me realize how good I have it at home, or even encouraged me to see a way I might try to improve my own hometown. It is always eye-opening.

By now, the flight was almost over. We were about to land, and Mona was once again holding her hands over her ears. I knew the minute the door opened she would pounce on the teacher, once again, to make sure he remembered her message and make sure that the boy that *built the door* got it. I felt really bad for him.

I knew he would be fair game at the luggage carousel. None of the boys seemed to have much carry-on baggage, so it was inevitable they would all end up there—waiting for bags—with Mona, hearing about *the key to their future*. I could just imagine her counseling the whole group of boys while watching the carousel.

I was torn. I kind of wanted to go and stand nearby and listen—to be a fly on the wall. I knew it would be good and full of drama, but I also wanted to get home, and there was the off chance she might corner *me* rather than the teacher.

Frankly, that was one trip I was not willing to take.

I WANT TO BE A PART OF IT

It was my first trip back to New York since the COVID-19 outbreak and I was stunned by the quiet. It's usually so noisy there. Coming from a small town you really notice that. But this time it was noticeably quiet. Eerily quiet.

I think it was the reduction in traffic. People were back on the sidewalks and tourists were out and about, but the traffic was definitely less. I wasn't hearing any horns and not many sirens. Had COVID made everyone nicer? More patient? Not feeling the need to honk? I don't know. I just know that every time I left my hotel, I noticed the difference.

When I tell people I am going to New York—again—they will often argue that they don't like New York because it is too busy, the traffic is too congested, the sidewalks are too crowded, and so on. I think they are trying to convince me that it's not worth all the trouble. And for them, I guess it would not be worth all the trouble. I feel differently.

I chose to make this trip back to New York—during a still-active pandemic—to support the thing that I love so much: theater. (Ok, the German chocolate cake has a lot to do with it too, but it's mainly the theater.)

I don't think a lot of people really understand the

scope of theater and the arts in New York. I know I didn't. Growing up I guess I thought that there was *one* Broadway theater where all these shows originated. I thought it might be like the touring companies that come to town for a week and then leave, with another show stopping-in a few weeks later. I could not fathom, at a young age, that there were over forty Broadway theaters, with shows running in each one, all at the same time. I certainly could not imagine that many shows to choose from.

But what really blew my mind was that these forty-or-more shows running on Broadway did not include all the shows that are playing Off-Broadway or Off-Off-Broadway.

Broadway is an inclusive term for all the shows running in the forty theaters in the Theater District. These are the shows in the larger theaters—venues that hold more than five hundred patrons—housing all the famous musicals and plays that you hear about. Then, mixed in this area as well, you will find many of the Off-Broadway theaters. These are the theaters that have anywhere from one hundred to five hundred seats. Then there are the Off-Off-Broadway theaters —some in the Theater District and some in other parts of the city—and they are usually very small venues with less than a hundred seats.

The Off-Broadway theaters are often testing grounds for shows that will later make their way to Broadway, like *Hamilton* or *Dear Evan Hansen*. Some of these venues do house long-running shows too. Those could be shows that can't sell enough tickets to occupy a big theater, but are still selling tickets consistently, like *The Fantasticks* did for over forty years. The Off-Off-Broadway theaters house a lot of the more experimental works as well as workshops where playwrights can hone their scripts.

What is truly amazing to me about all of this is that, on any given night in NYC, you can easily have over a hundred live theatrical works to choose from. There is really nothing quite like it.

Over the years, I have learned more and more about the years of work, collaboration, and trial-and-error that go into putting a show on a legendary Broadway stage. It is not for the faint of heart. It's not easy for the writers, the producers, the cast, or anyone involved. It's a multi-million-dollar roll of the dice that usually ends up craps. It's no more a guaranteed success for Stephen Sondheim or Andrew Lloyd Webber than it is for the new kid on the block making his first attempt.

I've watched so many documentaries and read so many biographies (it's a hobby of mine) about the great minds of the theater, and I tip my hat to them all. I am constantly amazed at the lives these composers, writers, directors, and actors have lived. It seems they have accomplished so much in their lifetimes. They have the same twenty-four hours in a day as I do, but they seem to produce so much more. What they do is like catching lightening in a bottle: an almost impossible feat and yet, when they do get it right, it is glorious.

One of the main things I've learned from all these biographies I read is that most of the really successful creative people seemed to have learned at an early age to pursue their passions and interests with blinders on. They focus in on what is important and block out the doubters and the naysayers. I think this is important in any profession, but especially when your work is artistic or subjective and might only appeal to a limited audience. You have to find your inner voice, and stay true to it. You have to be confident that your work is of value. It takes big risks to have big payoffs.

I have never been much of a risk-taker. I have always been one to err on the side of caution. I would not offer this as advice to any young person. Instead I would say that it's easier to take chances when you are young. So do it.

I'd like to think, in another life, I might be designing sets or costumes on Broadway. Or maybe even writing a show. I guess, technically, I am still not too old to do those things in this life, but I know that the odds are getting slimmer and slimmer with each passing day.

I grew up thinking that the people who performed on Broadway were extra-special. I couldn't imagine they were the kind of people who would grow up in Boonetown. So I never let myself think that I could work in that world, or on that level.

But then, in 1989, I was in my living room in Boonetown watching TV as Michael Jeter accepted the Tony Award for his performance in the hit Broadway production of *Grand Hotel*. He was born and raised just a few blocks from me in Boonetown. I never knew him because he had moved away before I got to high school, but I saw his dad almost every morning in the Boonetown post office.

So there. I guess it *was* possible. Someone from Boonetown could make it big on Broadway and even beyond. He went on to win Emmy Awards and be nominated for an Oscar. Yes, it was possible. Not probable, but possible. That possibility was always there, I guess, in the back of my mind, but I still never let myself think that I could be a part of that world. It just seemed too big.

And even if I did have the talent to make it as a set designer or something less grand, would I have had the stomach for it? New York is the place that separates the men from the boys. You have to be tough. Making these shows come to life eight times a week requires gifted individuals that somehow manage to survive a life in the theater: the rejection, the poverty, the hope, and the hopelessness.

And we don't even see the work happening backstage. That's an entire show in itself.

What we do see is the cast of working actors, living out their dream performing on Broadway. They are wildly-talented, hard-working individuals that mold themselves into a wide variety of characters in order to keep a job and exist doing something they love. They are the worker-bees that go on eight times a week performing a role that someone else, with a known name, created in the original Broadway cast and then left, after a year or so, to pursue other roles.

They are the Mormons, and the Elphabas, and the Phantoms that we have never heard of until we take our seat at a hit show that has been running long past the contract dates of the original cast. And they are the lucky ones. They are the ones who are working, the ones who are able to keep a job in the theater. For every individual on stage, there are hundreds and hundreds of others trying to get their part. It is a hard, competitive life.

Christine Pedi is a good example. Most people have probably never heard of her. She has spent her life as a working actor-singer-impressionist and is brilliantly talented. Now, one of her part-time jobs is as a disc-jockey on the Sirius Broadway channel. That's how I found out about her.

For decades, though, she has performed nightly in Off-Broadway shows like *Forbidden Broadway* and *Newsical: The Musical*. She is also a well known cabaret performer. But her real claim-to-fame is her amazing impressions. They are so good it's scary. It's hard to believe anyone can mimic so many people so well. But even with all this talent, she has never achieved household name status.

I have seen her in her cabaret performances several times, and I am constantly astounded at her abilities. She's just so damn funny. It's theater-insider humor, and I get it. The joy she has brought me is immeasurable. I've heard her say more than once that it's a hard life, but it is obvious that she loves her craft.

Even with loads of talent, there are no guarantees for actors, producers, directors, or investors. One of the best examples is the subject of a documentary, *Best Worst Thing that Ever Could Have Happened*, about the making of the show *Merrily We Roll Along*.

Hal Prince was already a legend in the Broadway world as the producer and/or director of such hits as *The Pajama Game, Damn Yankees, Fiddler on the Roof, West Side Story, She Loves Me, Company, and Cabaret*.

Stephen Sondheim was equally as pedigreed with critically acclaimed successes as lyricist and/or composer for shows like *West Side Story, Gypsy*,

Company, Follies, A Little Night Music, and *Sweeney Todd.* So when they chose their next project to work on together, everyone expected a hit. How could it not be, with two certified geniuses at the helm? *Merrily We Roll Along* closed after sixteen performances. Everyone involved was devastated, especially the young cast, most of whom were in their first show.

If you love theater, I highly recommend this documentary. It beautifully explores the complexity of making magic: sometimes it's there and sometimes it is not. Even with a score filled with great songs, the show did not work. Stephen and Hal never worked together again—another tragedy of that experience.

There are no "sure things" in theater. Not even for the best of the best. Not even for two geniuses. Every single time, you brace yourself, you grit your teeth and pray you roll a seven.

This is why I love New York City so much. It is a community of people living for their art. A modern-day bohemia.

There are so many other reasons to love New York too.

Iconic venues with stunning architecture, like Radio City Music Hall and Carnegie Hall, come to mind. I am amazed by the beauty of Grand Central Station, and I always enjoy walking through Central Park. I love spending days out exploring little shops and restaurants that have their own personality, and I love the happy accidents when you find a cool new shop or gallery.

At home in Boonetown, I used to run into this man at antique auctions. We had a lot of similar interests and he was fascinating to talk to. Over the years, we became friends and I'd often bump into him at lunch and we would have a chat. The subject of hats came up one day—he had an extensive collection—and I asked him where he found his. He went into great detail about a little hat shop in New York where he bought all his hats. He told me all about the area where the shop was located and how many hats he had purchased there over the years. I wasn't surprised. This man had a worldly air about him, and I figured he traveled a lot. He said they had a huge inventory and he felt sure that they would have hats to fit me.

I asked him how often he went to New York, and I was stunned when he said he had never been. He said he just called the store and they shipped the hats to him. It really made me kind of sad. I felt that he was missing the whole experience of shopping in New York.

But, you see, that's the thing about New York: it is so ingrained in our culture—especially in our television shows and films—that people everywhere, even those who have never been there, feel a part of it.

One day I was out walking on the Upper West Side and happened upon the very hat shop my friend had told me about. I stopped in.

It was Easter Sunday and I was surprised they were open. I had just left the Easter Parade on Fifth Avenue. (Yes, they still have the Easter Parade, but it's a little more outrageous than the one in the movie of the same name.)

Accidentally walking into the *Easter Parade*—where people were sporting elaborate two- and three-foot-tall hats made from bird cages, umbrellas, flower pots, and even old-time-cash-registers—was another memorable New York moment. But, the fact that no one had even mentioned it to me was also so very New York. Had this been happening in my hometown, it would have been advertised for months in advance and touted as a major tourist attraction. There, in New York, it was just another event, in a city full of interesting events. It went largely unnoticed and was barely mentioned.

I was happily surprised that this shop had many hats in extra-extra-large that fit me just fine. I bought a couple. While I was checking out, a man came in, a rather robust gentleman, in a bright-royal-blue, three-piece suit, accented with an equally bright lemon-yellow tie, worn with a white dress shirt. The man was not wearing a hat, and he was in a hurry. I think he was on his way to church, or maybe he was late for the Easter Parade. Anyway, I stuck around to see what he bought. He asked the clerk if they had a hat to match his suit. I was thinking, *Are you kidding?* No one would have a hat to match that suit.

The clerk studied him a bit and went into the back room. They had a huge inventory, but still this was an odd request. Imagine my utter shock when the clerk popped out of the back room, less than five minutes later, with a royal-blue straw hat, that was not only the exact shade as his suit, but also had a lemon-yellow accent band around it. It was a perfect match.

The customer put on the hat, smiled and said, "I'll take it." Well, of course he would, it looked like it had been ordered to match his ensemble. If the clerk had taken longer in the back, I would have thought he was dying a hat to match. The fact that it was a perfect fit was the icing on the cake. This implied to me that the store carried this color hat in a variety of sizes, which was even more mind-boggling.

Over in the Fashion District one day, I stumbled upon a button store. It was enchanting. Every shelf was filled with boxes that were about the size of a shoebox, except only an inch or so tall. On the end of each box, there would be five or six sample buttons of one design. They would start out in the smallest size and make their way up to the largest size button, representing the inventory in the box. There were buttons made of every kind of material and every shape and color imaginable. Each shelf probably had a hundred boxes of buttons, and there were hundreds and hundreds of shelves.

I couldn't help but think about all the costume designers who have stopped in to select just the right buttons to finish off a garment. A garment that would evoke a period or a style and bring a character to life on a Broadway stage. I loved the feel of that place.

That's the thing about New York. As many times as you roam the same streets and neighborhoods, there will always be something new to discover. Something unusual, something amazing, or even something ordinary, but *something*.

I thought I had found the best German chocolate cake anywhere at one of the famous bakeries there. Then one day, strolling down Ninth Avenue, I discovered Amy's Breads. I tried their German chocolate cake and found a new favorite. Always discovering.

On some days, I just want to re-visit my favorite old places, like the New York Public Library. Not to check out any books. I go there to bask in the architecture. I want to feel the proportions and study the materials. It's breathtaking. I still discover new things. The last time I was there, I noticed that each of the stairwells have different ceiling designs. One has an elaborately detailed dome shape, one has elongated arches, and the largest staircase has a huge skylight built into sort of a tray ceiling. It's delicious food for a design geek such as myself. It also makes me a bit melancholy knowing that nothing like this will ever be built again. It's just too expensive.

I recently found out that there have been additions, over the years, to house their massive collection. I figured the overflow books were stored off-site somewhere, but I was wrong. I learned that the additions were built underground, under Bryant Park located behind the library. It's quite ingenious: huge bunkers with aisles and aisles of books. And they are not shelved traditionally, by the old Dewey Decimal System. Instead, they are shelved by size so there isn't an inch of space wasted. Many cities would have just stuck some big modern addition on the back of the building. Not New York. Nice touch.

Usually by late afternoon, after a long day of walking and exploring, my legs are tired and my feet are hurting, so I head back to the hotel for some rest, and then end the day with a trip to the theater.

What makes theater really great is hard to explain. For me, it is found in a moment or a song which so perfectly captures a character's emotion that you are transported into that person's world, and you understand them.

A show that was unexpectedly full of such moments was *Grey Gardens*. Christine Ebersole gave a Tony-Award-winning, tour-de-force performance that I've never forgotten. I even went back to New York to see it again, just to make sure it was as good as I remembered.

It was even better.

The eleven o'clock number, *Another Winter in a Summer Town,* is such a perfectly written and performed lyric that you could not only hear a pin drop in the theater, you could actually feel her heart break as she sang. By the end of the song, tears were rolling down her face as they were for many in the audience.

Not every show can do that, bring out that much emotion. But, at every show, there is the *potential* to experience something this special. Knowing that is what keeps me coming back.

So, yes, all of you who say the city is too crowded and too noisy are correct. Some parts of New York City are dirty, and some parts of the city smell bad. New York is blistering hot in the summer and bitter cold in the winter. The traffic is horrendous and the subways are packed. The hotel rooms are expensive and they are small.

There are so many reasons to avoid it.

As for me, I can't wait to go back—and be a part of it.

SUDDENLY, A WRITER

When I published the book, *Shoes and Cheese: The Boonetown Chronicles,* I had no idea what I was doing. I feel pretty sure I did everything wrong, but it was a huge learning experience.

It just sort of happened. By accident. I was just writing down stories I've told a million times, and sharing them with friends during the COVID lockdown. Then, with a lot of encouragement from those friends, I decided to put my stories together in a book. It's all their fault really. They were the ones that planted the *book* seed. I really hadn't ever considered it before. I'm not mad at them or anything —actually just the opposite. It's been one of the most fun things I've ever done.

But now, there are some expectations.

People want me to do *more* things that I have never done, like have readings—which bring on a whole lot of anxiety even though they can also be a lot of fun—and do book signings.

And I kind of feel like an imposter because I still don't think of myself as a writer. A storyteller, maybe.

Whatever the words, the experience has taken me way outside of my comfort zone, and maybe that's a good thing.

I'm often surprised by some of the comments people make about my book. This one friend of mine, a writer himself, said he a found a serious subtext in my essay *The Bathroom Pro's*. He felt I was making a comment on humanity and how we humans really are all alike.

I assured him that, no, it really is just a story about the day two former pro-wrestlers ended up in my bathroom at the same time. I just thought it was a funny coincidence. He continued to protest. "No," he said, "I can see a deeper meaning and, as the reader, it is my choice to see what I want in your writing."

I guess he was right, it is his choice, but it still made me feel a little fake.

The simple fact is that I am not a literary type. I mean, I do like to read, but mostly biographies of composers and writers and directors and such—all related to theater, of course. Saying that I am well-read would be a vast overstatement.

I always *intend* to read many more books than I actually do. I have many books on my bedside table, waiting to be picked up, but they are gathering dust.

I hated reading in grade school, high school and college. I think the teachers and professors searched far and wide to find the most boring books possible to assign for book reports.

I wasn't raised in a family of readers and that was a big part of my problem. It just didn't seem normal to me to sit around the house and read. My parents always read the newspaper, but never books. In their defense, they didn't have much free time. I did. I just didn't like to spend it reading.

Actually, I prefer to listen to books. Since I drive so much, it makes great use of the time. And I love hearing an author read their own work. It feels a little bit like cheating, but I think this is just carry-over guilt associated with reading *CliffsNotes* in college rather than actually reading the assigned book.

In my own defense, being assigned *David Copperfield* with about two thousand excruciatingly boring pages did nothing to make me want to read. I think this was a case of a college professor exerting his power over a bunch of uninterested freshmen. "I'll show them," he thought. (Incidentally, *David Copperfield* was the book that made me first turn to *CliffsNotes* for help.)

Another thing I have noticed since I published my book is that it seems *everyone* wants to, or is thinking about, writing a book. I had no idea.

I guess this makes my publishing books all the more ironic, since I had *never* thought about writing a book. I had dabbled with playwriting, but I had never given any thought to publishing a book.

One day while at the deli having lunch, the stock broker, who often sits at a table near me, heard me talking about the publication date for my book. He began to tell me all about the book he planned to write. Apparently, by day he was a business-casual stockbroker, but during his vacation time he became a big game hunter, traveling the world to shoot hippos and rhinos. He talked about being in Africa, in the jungle, and living in a tent with twenty or so locals who would skin the rhino after he shot the poor thing and harvest the meat. I was pretty stunned by the whole encounter.

He was quite excited about the fact that he and his

guide had gotten into some sort of misunderstanding, or altercation, with the locals. It was about the compensation they were to pay for their help with the dead animal. At one point he said he feared for his life. It was definitely an interesting story. One I suppose many hunters would love.

I told him right then *not* to buy my book. I couldn't really see him finding my stories very interesting after hearing him talk about his travels and these adventurous hunts. I wasn't sure I'd find his book interesting either. Hunting stories aren't really my thing. But that's what makes the world go round, isn't it?

Without a doubt, the scariest thing about publishing a book—for me—is that *anyone* in the world can read it. Once it's published, it's out there in the world for everyone. People that you like or dislike, or have absolutely nothing in common with, will judge your work, whether you are ready or not.

You have to be ready to take criticism from anyone that wants to dish it out. It's a bit risky. Especially when the topic is you. And you have to be willing to live with what you publish from now on. The pages are not written with disappearing ink. So, the reader can go back to them as many times as they like—now or in the future.

In fact, I was kind of embarrassed at first, to share my crazy thoughts. But back during the COVID shutdown (before the vaccine) everyone was desperate for entertainment. So I decided I would read a few stories I had written to some friends. We could all sit on my patio, with plenty of space between us, and feel relatively safe as I told tales of my hometown and my life.

And guess what?

They laughed.

They laughed a lot.

A ham was born.

When I realized that my stories could brighten someone's day and change someone's mood, that's when I knew I wanted to write more. So I did.

As I began to seriously consider publishing my stories, and to really work at writing, I felt as if I was back to square one. I really had no confidence in my work and no idea how it would be received. It was terrifying actually. What kept me going was having people that believed in me.

We creative types are a sensitive lot. It took me years to feel confident in my design work. In the beginning, I would never strongly assert my opinions for fear of being criticized or judged. But years of experience give you confidence. Now I will stand firm and fight for my choices. None of that assurance came along for the ride when I started writing.

Many of my friends had confidence in me as a writer long before I did. They believed in me from those first readings and never wavered. That made me want to work hard and make them proud. I've thought about that a lot throughout this process. It has only made me realize, more than ever, how important it is to tell creative people when you enjoy their work. It feeds them. Especially when they are starting out. It gives them the encouragement they need to keep going.

I revealed a lot about myself in my stories. A lot of

the things I talked about were things I had been so self-conscious of in my youth, and yet, here I was, putting it all out there for anyone in the world to read.

I had no idea what to expect and no idea if I would sell any books. And I worried how people would perceive it. I didn't know if people would get my humor, or my storytelling style, or relate to it at all.

When I published my book in the fall of 2021, we were still in the midst of COVID-19, so it was done with little fanfare, but the notes and calls were all I needed. I got texts and messages from lots of people I knew, but also from lots of people I had never met, people who knew nothing about me or my hometown. They got my humor too.

As it turns out, small-town humor is pretty much universal.

My friends told me they were really proud of me for taking the chance and for what I had done. I'll be honest, I was pretty proud of me too.

Amazing really, when I think about it. I suppose I am a writer now.

THEN AND NOW

I remember turning forty and thinking I was old.
I remember turning fifty and thinking I was old.
Now I am sixty.
All of a sudden, I realize that I am now officially "vintage". It seems everywhere I go someone is introducing a new line of this or that with a "vintage" look—I suppose to evoke an era—that will appeal to young buyers and some sentimental old buyers too. I see this in clothes mostly, but just the other day I was selecting new frames for my eyeglasses and it suddenly hit me that I have worn every single style on the rack, at one point or another, during my life. Wire frames, plastic frames, aviators, preppy, dorky, big, small, round, or rectangular, I have had them all and have the photos to prove it.

Adidas just introduced a new line of "classic" tennis shoes—that I wore in high school. Both styles. Apparently, they are now so old that they are back in style. One pair had the three blue stripes (that I wore when I was a freshman), and the other pair was white with the green tab at the heel (those were my sophomore year). I kind of wish I still had both of those, to be honest.

Designer décor that I wanted desperately for my

bedroom in my teens is also now back in style and, incidentally, very expensive. So much of what I loved—and so much of what I loathed—has come back around.

So I find myself in an interesting place. I am way past middle-aged, but I don't feel old. It's an odd place to be.

I am still young enough to *really* love my iPhone, yet old enough to remember my grandmother's party line.

Grandma lived in the rural part of southern Tennessee, near Boonetown. My first memories of her house and her party-line phone would have been in the late 1960s, when I was around six or seven years old. She hadn't had *any* phone service at her rural home for most of her life, so having a phone, even if it was a party-line, was new technology for her.

I don't mean *party* in the fun way either.

I mean party like *party-of-eight* when you are asking for a large table a restaurant. Back then, she shared a line with six other homes. Can you imagine that now? Telling someone they would have to share their cell service with a group of random people would surely cause immediate heart failure.

But Grandma was thrilled to have her phone. She didn't seem to mind having to wait until no one else was on their phone to make a call. And she often had others listen in on her calls. I'm not sure when she finally got her own dedicated line, but I think it was in the late 1980s or early '90s.

She also still had an outhouse. They had gotten indoor plumbing when I was in grade school. But I remember the outhouse. I never used it, but Grandpa still did.

I cannot imagine what my grandparents would have thought of cell phones or any of the gadgets we have today—I'm sure it would blow their minds.

Many of the topics I've been writing about recently involve all the changes I have seen take place in my lifetime. It makes me a bit nostalgic. Would I want to give up all the new technology and go back? Well, no. But it's still pretty overwhelming when I think about it.

I feel the world has changed more in the last twenty-five years than at any other time in history. That's about how long the internet has been widely available, and the iPhone was only introduced fifteen years ago. Just think about that—apps have only been around *fifteen* years.

At fifteen, I vividly remember wanting a push button telephone. This was the latest technology at the time. In the house where I grew up, we had two big, ugly, black phones with rotary dials. I would see, on one of our *four* television channels—that's right, I said four—all the new, colored, push-button phones available, and would whole-heartedly lust after them. They still had to be hard wired to the wall jack and were not portable, but the push-button feature seemed so advanced and so cool. I literally could not wait to dial someone by punching those buttons. My parents built a house when I was a senior in high school and we finally got three new phones, complete with push buttons, in various colors. I was so excited.

We got our first microwave oven in 1982. It was massive. Everything burned at first because we couldn't understand how it heated so fast. I'd hear friends talk about blowing breakers because they put metal pans in their new microwaves causing an explosion of sparks. It was quite hilarious to see all the melted containers too. But we didn't have Facebook then so no one could compare disasters.

At work, I bought our first fax machine sometime in the late 1980s. We simply could not believe it. Transmitting a piece of paper in seconds and not having to mail it overnight via FedEx seemed like the future. It was truly a miracle. People would come to our office to use our fax machine when they got in a bind and needed to get a document somewhere the same day. The only problem was not a lot of other people had fax machines when we first got ours. So, often we would have to find a third party, in the city we were transmitting to, that would receive the document for the person in need of the document. Our fascination with the fax machine didn't last all that long though — maybe a decade.

Then came the internet.

If you weren't alive before the internet, I don't think you can ever understand. It seemed to all happen so gradually — at first — and everyone kept saying, "What's the big deal? So, you can send e-mail. So what?"

Then all of a sudden, it seemed, everyone was totally dependent on it. And now, I don't think we really stop and appreciate it. Cell phones, of course, allowed people to communicate more easily while on the go, but cell phones could only connect one person to another. The internet could take you to the world, to people and places literally anywhere. No need to go to the library to do research and no need for a set of

World Book Encyclopedias at home. Anything you needed could be downloaded from the web. Suddenly no one was out of reach, and everything could be accessed immediately.

With all this new access though, the losses began. Favorite things from my childhood and teen years began to look like museum artifacts.

My grade-school album collection and high school collection of cassette tapes had already become relics and suddenly were not even yard-sale-able. My CD collection from my twenties and thirties is now in a drawer collecting dust. All my music is digital now.

I hate it.

I truly miss browsing for music at Tower Records and bringing home a new CD to enjoy for an evening. But I'll admit I don't miss a car full of CD cases sliding around in the floorboard.

I can't remember the last time I bought a full album of music. I thought I would never fall victim to downloading just one or two songs from an album, but I realize that I have. I used to love taking the "album journey" with one of my favorite musicians through their labor of love—their latest album. I wanted to understand their concept and intent and feel the connection of the songs.

Sadly, now, I just preview the new songs on my iPhone and only purchase the ones that hit me within that thirty-second sample. Even sadder, most music now seems to be reduced to little twenty-second clips on *TikTok*. It seems no one has the attention span to even listen to an entire song, much less a full album.

When my family went on vacation, we would each take along our Kodak cameras with several rolls of film, snapping pictures along the way. The quality was usually poor: blurred, lighting issues, a finger in the frame, or worse. We would hope for a few good shots. I say hope, because you really had no idea until you had the film developed and the pictures printed days or weeks after you returned home.

Then you took the best shots and put them together in a photo album, hoping some friends might stop by so you could show them your vacation pictures. It was always a big joke back in those days: boring your friends with your vacation photos or slides or videos. No one ever really wanted to see them. Good friends would kindly sit as you toured them, slowly, through each album and photo. They would *ooh* and *aah* as required, secretly hoping to escape.

But people don't need to make albums anymore and people don't need to stop by to see them. For that matter they don't stop by and visit unannounced anymore. Why would they? What could you possibly tell them about—in person—that they haven't already seen on your Facebook or Instagram page. Everyone has already posted their vacation photos, their children's accomplishments, and what they are having for dinner right there online for all to see.

Now, you can speed though your friends vacation photos, placing little hearts in the corner, indicating your interest and jealousy at a very quick pace, thus making your friend feel content that they have properly shown-off and rubbed-in their trip. You have literally seen their vacation unfold in real time on social media. You no longer have to spend the socially required amount of time actually looking at their vacation photos in person.

This might be one of the best benefits of social media.

These days, many of my friends have Apple watches. So far, I have refused. I love my iPhone and almost have a panic attack if I can't find it or leave it somewhere, but I don't want to be *that* connected. I resent how much time I spend on my phone, and yet I can't put it down. I guess the phone isn't convenient enough for a lot of people, and they want a watch that keeps them even more connected to everyone and everything.

A couple of new young friends of mine now have rings that are bluetoothed to their phone. These rings look like a simple wedding band but will monitor their heart rate, remind them to get up and move around, and alert them to text messages. It makes me wonder what is coming next.

I have a feeling I know.

As a matter of fact, I feel sure it has already been invented. I fully believe, within my lifetime, we will have the option to have a chip implanted in our body that will take the place of our cell phones. You will be able to say a command and all of a sudden you will hear Aunt Mary speaking out of your chest, or maybe your armpit.

Of course, it will be introduced first by Apple as the new "iChip" and young people will be waiting in lines like never before to get this new iChip implanted. Instead of waiting in line at the cell phone store though, you will have to queue-up at the walk-in clinic for minor surgery.

I feel like they will eventually devise a way to allow us to hear music, or the person on the other end of a phone call, internally, so that everyone on the sidewalk won't hear our music choices and private conversations, and we will no longer need earbuds. But I feel that those advances won't take place until we have the iChip2 or iChip3.

Personally, I am going to wait until at least the iChip3. I don't want to take any chances that an early version might malfunction. For instance, what if my snoring sounds like someone's name. The name Suzie, kind of sounds like an exhale to me. *Sooo-zeeee.* So, as I am falling off into a good sleep, I might exhale and accidentally call Suzie, only to be awakened by an angry friend wanting to know why in the hell I have called her at two in the morning. I'd be hearing all this craziness through my chest speaker and trying to figure out if I am nuts, or dreaming, but then I'd finally realize it's coming from the iChip.

Or you might be having a private conversation about the torrid affair a friend is having, all while sending that very person the entire conversation via iChip messenger.

Yes, I will definitely wait for iChip3. I want to be sure the bugs are worked out.

We are already implanting chips in humans and in our pets for medical and tracking purposes, so why not for communication. It's coming—just wait.

All of this only makes our traditional means of communication and gathering news seem more and more antiquated. I used to love reading the local paper. I also loved looking at my design magazines. I could not wait for them to arrive each month. I can't remember the last time I looked at a copy of the Boonetown Times. I thought I would be one of the last holdouts, still reading the actual paper until their demise, but I gave in to convenience. I read all my news on my iPhone now.

I don't even watch television news anymore.

I think the locals have moved on from the newspaper too. There used to be all kinds of ads in the classifieds for yard sales and various services. Now we have Facebook Marketplace and online exchange sites.

I shouldn't complain too much about the internet. There are some really good things on there. There is one site, hosted by someone in Boonetown, that allows locals to ask for help if they need it, or give away things they are no longer using. Readers are also are encouraged to advertise helpful services.

This one particular ad turned out to be really popular with the readers. I never really thought about it as a needed service before, but I now see that it is.

It read: "Find a deceased pet that's fresh? You can bring it to me. I will freeze it until the owners are located! I will also make posts in all groups, check for chips (if you haven't), use pet websites, etc. I do take not-so-fresh pets, but their skeleton will be cleaned and bagged for those who do not want to bury their baby. They'll also have any form of description I can pick up off them…"

Readers expressed so much appreciation, many of them were comforted just knowing this service was available.

Lots of users on the site offer free furniture and clothes to others in need. One reader was offering a free sofa and loveseat. They said the only thing wrong was a hole in the back of the loveseat. They had to cut it open to get out their pet snake.

The internet is a great way for people to share

information and it can bring people together in many good ways. But I think it can also make people feel isolated. If you don't participate in social media sites, you are out of the loop of many friends and relatives.

If you do participate in social media, you can easily get caught in the mindset that your life isn't much to brag about or that you aren't doing enough with your time. We all know that many of the users on social media sites wildly exaggerate and use Photoshop to make it *appear* they are living a dream life. But still, it's hard not to feel like you are the dull and lonely one when all your friends appear to be out having a blast.

Sometimes I feel that all this social media and technology keeps me up to date and somewhat relevant. Other days, not so much.

I often feel like I am just barely keeping up—with technology that is—really showing my age, so to speak. Sometimes I think that any day I will be as obsolete as last years iPhone.

I try to take it all with a grain of salt. Does it really matter if I know what the latest apps can do, or if I can use them? Not really. I just don't want to feel completely left behind. I don't want to feel that old—yet.

I guess every generation feels that way—like new ideas are leaving them behind—as they age. I know my parents did. My mom and dad struggled to keep up with the technology of their day, just like I am now with current technology. They were never able to program their VCR (video cassette recorder) to record a show, or even set the clock. Even though they wanted to watch movies and videos of their grandkids, it wasn't something they would try to learn. I don't know how many times I set the clock for them.

In their defense, programming one of the early VCR's to record a program did require a degree in astrophysics. But they resisted other new technology as well. I think it was a combination of not caring and just being tired of learning new things.

I totally get that.

There is one thing I actually like about aging. It is something I think my parents came around to and their parents too. I like to call it, for lack of a better phrase, "Not giving a damn."

"Giving a damn" is something I have spent way too much time on. I think most of us probably have. More specifically, I've spent way too much time giving a damn about what people think. Should I really care if young people think I am old and out of touch? No. Not at all.

Thankfully, as you age, you learn that people don't think about you nearly as much as you think they do.

And, even if they do, what does it matter? The younger you are when you have this realization, the better. Because the way I see it, at the end of the day, all that *really* matters is what you think of yourself.

And if you are lucky enough to have people in your life that think about you for the *right* reasons and genuinely worry about your happiness and health, you are indeed fortunate. If people are thinking about you for other reasons, I think they probably have too much time on their hands, and they need to get a life of their own.

The older I get, the more I realize that there is way

too much to do and too much of this world to see to worry about anyone else's opinions. Aging just reinforces this way of thinking in me.

I realize now how precious time is.

I prioritize.

That's what I am trying to do as I get older. Focus on what makes me happy and ignore the negative. I think that's great advice. I hope I take it.

THE END

I have been with several loved ones as they were dying. I consider it a great privilege. Being with someone who was there when I came into the world seems to complete the circle of life.

While that is not where anyone necessarily *wants* to be, I call it a privilege because I think there is no greater moment of need—and no greater thing one can do—than to comfort someone as they transition from this world. I think it is the most grown-up thing we can ever do.

In my cases, the people I sat beside were older and had, for the most part, lived long happy lives. So while seeing them pass away was sad, it was not devastating like seeing someone die young, or losing someone in a tragic accident.

These end-of-life experiences have usually occurred after a long string of difficult decisions involving medical care, nursing homes, resuscitation directives, hospice, and so on. It isn't easy on the care-giver or the patient, but when your time comes, you just hope that someone will be there to make those decisions in a respectful and compassionate way. And hopefully, dying will be peaceful, with dignity, and without pain. But what happens after that?

In several interviews with Betty White that aired after her death, she would say, after a loved one's death, "Now they know the secret." And now she does too.

But what is the secret?

I think every religion has their interpretation of what the afterlife is. Maybe every individual does too. But no one seems to have a clear idea of what it might be like on a day-to-day basis. I think most of us believe we will change forms in some way or another.

My question has always been: Do we change into another type of entity altogether? Or do we achieve some kind of human perfection?

Do the lifelong dieters finally achieve their goal weight...and stay there?

Does my dad finally have the beautiful singing voice he always thought he had?

If I finally have athletic ability to go with my height, will I have to spend the afterlife playing basketball? Please God, no.

Will you be the younger version of yourself, or the older and wiser one?

Maybe we will look the way we always wanted to look—like what we thought was perfect here on earth. If that is so, I'm afraid there will be a lot of Charlize Therons, Halle Berrys, and George Clooneys roaming around somewhere up there. The first few weeks of that would be fun, I admit. But after a while, would you get bored with all that gorgeousness?

Or maybe—finally—we would see the beauty in each of us that was there all along.

Whatever happens, I hope we at least retain our own

individual personalities. I think we will need something to set us apart.

And what would we do all day?

Surely there are no illnesses, and no one will have to work. So how do you pass the time? You wouldn't need to go to doctor's appointments, and there would be no need to take vacations because you literally are *in Heaven.* There would be nowhere better to go.

I guess, since everyone would be available, we could just have concerts every day. I could see all the classic Broadway shows I missed. The casts would be right there on hand. That would be amazing. And, I could finally see *Judy Garland Live at Carnegie Hall.* Poor thing, she would probably have to relive that concert at least monthly—*everyone* wanted to be there at that original, legendary show.

Though I am afraid even that could get repetitive after a while.

And all the frustrated sports fans, I suppose, could now play pro-level ball anytime they wanted.

But who would win? Everyone would be equally great.

Of course, when you first arrive in the afterlife, you could spend a lot of time catching-up with parents and grandparents and loved ones that preceded us in death. But it seems like that wouldn't take an eternity. And we are there for eternity, right?

What will we do for the next few eons?

One of my teachers in grade school, a nun, once told me that Heaven would be like the best day we ever had on earth—except every single day. That's a nice thought.

The End

But what are we wearing?

Will we still have bodies that need clothes, or are we just romping around naked all day? We will all surely be beautiful and well-toned, so the naked thing might work well, but I feel like I will still want to make a fashion statement in the afterlife.

And, incidentally, will I finally be able to buy clothes off the rack? I mean that has always kind of seemed like Heaven to me. Buying clothes that fit, right off the rack. I can't really let myself think about that too much though, I get a little light headed.

On the other hand, what if we don't retain our human form?

What if we become some sort of *aura* with an angelic spirit? If that is the case, what will we do all day?

Will we just sit around on a cloud — and *glow*?

Or maybe strum our harp?

I hate to say it, but that seems pretty boring to me.

If there is anything I have learned in writing, it is that any good plot needs tension and some discord to be interesting. I know it might sound ungrateful, but I think, even in the afterlife, I would like a little excitement now and then. Being perfect might get old.

Then there is that whole line of thinking that you might be sent back to earth now and then to straighten out things that you messed up while you were there. If that is the case, air traffic controllers will be very busy: there will be a lot of return visits.

Maybe things won't be so boring after all.

I guess none of us will ever know the secret, at least for now anyway.

And that's ok.

The End

It does help create the tension a good plot needs.

The one thing we do know for sure is that the final ending for each of us will be death.

And someone will bring ham.